"She openeth her mouth with wisdom; and
in her tongue is the law of kindness."

—PROVERBS 31:26 (KJV)

WHISTLE STOP
Café
= MYSTERIES =

WAIT TILL THE SUN SHINES

MARGARET WELCH

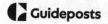

Published by Guideposts
100 Reserve Road, Suite E200
Danbury, CT 06810
Guideposts.org

Cover and interior design by Müllerhaus
Cover illustration by Greg Copeland, represented by Illustration Online LLC.
Typeset by Aptara, Inc.

ISBN 978-1-961251-92-2 (hardcover)
ISBN 978-1-961251-93-9 (epub)

Printed and bound in the United States of America
10 9 8 7 6 5 4 3 2 1

WAIT TILL
THE SUN
SHINES

CHAPTER ONE

It looks like every kid's idea of a treasure chest." Janet Shaw, her eyes wide, took in the size of the antique box with its arched top. "Do you know how Ian would describe it?" she asked, speaking of her police chief husband.

"I'm all ears," Kim Smith said.

"It's big enough to hide a body."

Kim laughed. "If it held a body, trust me, I would have invited Ian instead of you and Debbie." Kim, director of the Dennison Depot Museum, had asked her good friends Janet and Debbie, co-owners of the café situated in the depot, to come feast their eyes on the contents of the box. Janet had arrived in the museum workroom first. "Where's Debbie?" Kim asked. "Should we wait for her?"

Janet was itching to peek inside but said, "She'll be here any minute. After church, she and her parents joined the residents of Good Shepherd for Sunday lunch." Until he'd retired, Debbie Albright's father had been the director of Good Shepherd Retirement Center in Dennison. "Did someone really drop this beauty at the museum and say, 'Here. Have a treasure chest'?" Janet asked.

"Pretty much," Kim said. "But not to burst your bubble—it's technically a steamer trunk."

"But you said it has treasure in it," Debbie said as she bounced through the door. "I'm all agog."

"I can now give you the official details." Kim took a paper from her pocket. "Twenty-nine inches high in the center of the lid. Thirty-four long and twenty-two deep. The hardware is brass. The handles on each side are leather. The black slats on the top and sides are... I don't know what kind of wood. Maple or oak, maybe."

Janet walked around the trunk. "It conjures all kinds of stories about romantic foreign travel, doesn't it? I wish it had destination stickers all over it. Any idea how old it is? Who donated it?"

"I can answer one of those questions with confidence," Kim said. "A woman named Dawn Anderson. She isn't local, but she's been in town off and on over the last few months clearing out a deceased in-law's house. She was here when that television crew came to town to film for the *Days of Yesteryear* show."

"Gotcha," Janet said. "She caught the same bug everyone else did and hoped the trunk was more special than it is."

Debbie patted the trunk. "I think you're special even if the TV people turned up their noses."

"Mrs. Anderson said she wasn't surprised the TV people didn't exclaim over the contents," Kim said. "She thought the museum might be interested in them, though. I thanked her for being community minded. Then I told her the museum would accept the donation, but only with the stipulation that we can dispose of any part of it that we can't use for the museum's collections. Again, she didn't seem disappointed."

"She doesn't want any of it back?" Janet asked.

"She says she's up to her eyeballs in stuff and 'so over' the idea of any more stuff," Kim said. "As for how old the trunk is, after a quick bit of research my guess is 1930s. But possibly '40s, considering what's inside."

"Which is?" Debbie asked. "I mean really, Kim, how long are you going to torture us?"

"Be tortured no longer." Kim, with her flair for dramatics, lifted the trunk's lid. "Voilà. We have an amazing assemblage of 1940s women's clothing."

"Ooh!" The exclamation came from Janet and Debbie at the same time.

"May we?" Janet mimed taking the clothes out and holding them up.

"Be my guest," Kim said. "Take them out and lay them on the worktable as you go. There are a few other things mixed in with the clothes, mostly toward the bottom, that I haven't looked at yet."

"How could you resist? I mean, look at this." Debbie held up a white cotton dress with a dirndl skirt. Three rows of red rickrack edged the square neckline and the cuffs of the short, puffy sleeves, and also outlined the shape of a faux apron on the skirt.

"There's all kinds of adorable things in the trunk," Kim said, "and I wanted to share the fun of discovery."

Janet held up a robin's-egg blue shirtwaist dress covered in large white polka dots.

"Can we keep them?" Debbie asked. "I mean the museum, not us."

"Although…" Janet batted her eyes, making Kim laugh.

"Sadly, nothing in the trunk fits the museum's collection policy. Even sadder, as much as I love 1940s styles, none of the clothes fit *me*. But…" Kim said, giving them a conspiratorial look.

"But what?" Debbie asked. She laid the white dirndl on the worktable and picked up a wool blazer and houndstooth wool skirt.

"But I can see that you're as smitten as I am. I hoped you would be, because I have an idea."

"Take the day off and play dress-up?" Janet took a pair of elbow-length white calfskin gloves from the trunk and held the soft leather to her cheek. "Please?"

"Better than that," Kim said. "Let's have a—"

"Fashion show!" Janet and Debbie said at the same time then looked at each other and laughed.

"Great minds," Kim said. "Exactly what I was thinking. We can charge a fee to attend and split the proceeds between the museum and the café."

"What a great way to beat the January doldrums," Debbie said.

"Perfect," Janet said. "But can we pull it together fast enough to have it this month?"

"Again, great minds," Kim said. "We wouldn't *have* to do it this month, but it'd be a wonderful draw. We know January weather in Ohio goes from iffy to icy in a blink. Not the best month to attract out-of-town visitors. But a fashion show would bring in locals too."

"Especially if we ask locals to model," Janet said.

"So why don't you look through the rest of the trunk," Kim said, "and make sure our rose-colored glasses aren't skewing our judgment. I'll be back in a few. I need to make a call."

Janet and Debbie took turns removing items from the trunk, bringing out dresses, skirts, blouses, trousers, a handknitted sweater, a few hats, two pairs of shoes, and several more pairs of gloves.

"Because a woman just wasn't dressed to go out if she didn't wear gloves," Janet said, adopting a prim pose.

"They weren't wearing those gloves when they stitched these." Debbie lifted a stack of what appeared to be unassembled quilt blocks out of the trunk. "How cool is this? Each square has a different name embroidered in the center of it."

Kim appeared in the doorway.

"Did you see these?" Debbie held up the squares. "Look how pretty they are."

"These were at the bottom?" Kim took the pieces. "I'm sure the fabric is cotton flour sacking. But how often do you see pristine quilt blocks from that period?"

Janet scooted closer. Each block was created with squares and rectangles of a printed fabric and squares and triangles of plain white cotton. The printed fabrics were a rainbow of colors and a variety of patterns—floral, striped, checkered, plaid. A white square sat at the center of each, bearing the signature of the stitcher. "Do you recognize any of the names?"

"Some of the embroidered handwriting isn't legible. But a few," Kim said. "They've passed, though."

"This reminds me of the time capsule we opened last year," Janet said. "Names and possessions from out of the past, each with a story."

"They're called signature quilts," Kim said, "and they have stories to tell. They were often made by a group of friends or church members as a going-away or wedding present." She fanned through more squares. "There ought to be a Bible verse or some kind of congratulations or farewell message on one of these. A date too." A frown line appeared between her eyebrows. She looked quickly through the two or three dozen blocks again then shook her head.

"That's disappointing," Janet said. "But we can give the blocks an approximate date from the names. Maybe the fabric too?"

"True." Kim brightened. "And because there are local names, that means these were probably made right here and the quilt was meant for someone in Dennison. It might be a fun project to locate any of the quilters still with us. Or relatives of those who've passed."

"Fun for a volunteer?" Debbie asked.

"For me," Kim said with a grin. "I love quilts even if I don't quilt, and I love this kind of social history."

"Try to find out why it wasn't finished," Janet said.

"It makes you wonder, doesn't it?" Kim asked. "A lot of work went into these blocks."

"It did," Janet said, "and why they never became a quilt might be an interesting part of their story." She watched Debbie take a tailored skirt and blouse from the trunk, and then took her turn. "Here's the last and possibly least, considering how worn the material is. Oh." She looked up. "It isn't clothes. Something's wrapped inside the material. Have you seen this, Kim?"

"I didn't even make it as far as the quilt blocks. I assume that's more flour sacking, though," she said, referring to colorful fabric made from feed and grain bags during World War II and earlier.

"This is as much fun as guessing a Christmas present." Janet lifted the wrapped bundle out of the trunk and ran her fingers all around the shape. "It feels like a small box." She gently shook the object. "There's something inside." She carefully unfolded the fabric. "Oh my. I think the cloth is—" She gently shook it out and held up a faded, mended, obviously much-loved and often-used apron made of yellow, red, gray, and white plaid fabric.

"It's darling!" Debbie said.

Janet let Debbie take the apron from her. While Debbie and Kim exclaimed over its somehow unfaded brightly colored binding, she examined the small box she'd unwrapped. A hen and a rooster, painted on the top, looked back at her. On the front face, written in black lettering, was a word dear to her heart—*Recipes*. She swung the hinged lid open to see dozens of recipe cards and immediately started flipping through them.

"Have you ever seen an apron pattern like this?" Kim asked. "Aren't most of yours sort of rectangular?" The apron she held up was all curves. The bottom edge, rather than cut straight across, was rounded like a smile. The top of the bib was another curve, made large enough so that instead of a strap or tie for behind the neck, the seamstress had simply cut a hole big enough for the cook's head to pop through.

"I never have," Debbie said. "Seems very retro. Not retro back then, I guess. The yellow and red are perfect for the café, don't you think? It's like it was made for our decor. Wouldn't it be fun to make a couple of aprons like it? Does anyone make reproduction flour sack fabric?"

"Someone must," Kim said. "I'll do an online search when I have a free moment. What's the box, Janet?"

"Something that might be even better than the apron." Janet held the box to her heart. "It's a file box. With handwritten recipes from dozens of women including…" She stopped, then continued with a hitch in her voice. "Including Faye Canby, my grandma. It's her recipe for dream bars. She made them when I was little. I haven't had one or thought of them in years. This is the first time I've ever seen the recipe written down."

"With a name like that, are they as dreamy as they sound?" Kim asked.

"As far as I remember."

"Do you recognize any other names?" Kim asked.

"Come see." Janet patted the floor next to her. No way was she handing the recipe box to someone else before she'd seen every card. They flipped through them together, laughing at some of the odd-sounding recipes, pointing out those they'd enjoyed or avoided at community potlucks. They only recognized a few of the contributors.

"There's no name that tells you who the box belonged to?" Kim asked.

Janet examined the box, inside and out. "Nothing." She quickly fanned back through the recipes. "Some of the cards have women's names on them, but not all. At a guess, the cards without names were written by the owner. Because who would bother to write their name on their own recipe?"

Janet looked up to see Debbie smoothing a small stack of papers. "What have you got, Debbie?"

"The sweetest notes," Debbie said. "They were tucked into one of the trunk's side pockets. They're written by two different people— on each note, one person wrote the first few words and a second wrote the rest."

"Person A and Person B," Janet said.

"Spoken like the wife of a police chief," Kim said.

Debbie sorted through the notes. "Sometimes Person A starts the note, and sometimes Person B does. Listen to this one. Person A writes, 'Have I told you lately,' and Person B writes, 'that I love you.'"

"That's charming," Janet said. "Read another."

"Person A writes, 'You're only,' and Person B writes, 'as pretty as you treat people.'"

"I like that one nearly as much," Kim said. "But it almost sounds like the beginning of a joke. How many people does it take to write a—how many words in that note?"

Debbie laughed and counted. "Eight. How many people does it take to write an eight-word note?"

"The paper's yellowed," Kim said. "Maybe the notes are left from a 1940s or '50s party game. One person starts and another person finishes a well-known saying."

"That could be fun," Janet said. "I'd play."

"Oh, but here's the best one so far." Debbie held up a note then read it. "Person A writes, 'You are,' and another person, not B, based on the handwriting—"

"Person C?" Janet supplied.

Debbie nodded and handed the note to Janet. "It seems to be a child just learning to print. Person A writes, 'You are,' and Person C prints, 'my sunshine.' You were right when you said we'd find all kinds of adorable stuff in the trunk, Kim. This note is *every* kind of adorable. Thanks for sharing this with us."

"But now we've reached the end, haven't we?" Kim sighed. "No more surprises, except that the bottom of the trunk is covered with awfully pretty flower-sprigged paper."

"This doesn't look right," Janet said. She reached inside and pressed a finger on the bottom where it met the side of the trunk. It gave a little at her touch.

"What do you mean?" Debbie asked.

Janet rapped her knuckles lightly in several places on the bottom inside the trunk. "It doesn't sound right either. Listen." Kim and Debbie leaned in as she rapped again. "I think it's a false bottom."

"There's a stub of ribbon in the back left-hand corner," Kim said. "See if you can get hold of it and pull."

Janet pinched the ribbon tightly and tugged. She felt resistance then movement and, with another tug, the bottom came away. Beneath lay a white box that fit perfectly into the hidden space.

"I did not see that coming," Kim said. "You found it, Janet. You open it."

"I will not say no to that." Janet took a deep breath and lifted the lid of the box. Whatever lay inside had been carefully wrapped in tissue paper. She just as carefully folded the tissue back, revealing a white dress.

"Do you think it's a wedding dress?" she asked. "It looks almost too pretty to take out of the box or touch."

"But should we anyway?" Debbie asked.

"Are you kidding? Of course," Kim said. She fished a pair of cotton museum gloves from a pocket. "With these."

"You do the honors." Janet moved aside and let Kim take over.

The dress Kim lifted from its nest of tissue paper took Janet's breath away. Tea length, with a pleated skirt, it had a fitted waist and bodice with lace and beads across the shoulders.

"Early '40s, I think," Kim said. "Stand up, Debbie." When she did, Kim held the dress up to her. "Like it was made for you. You should model this in the fashion show. Can't you see it, Janet?"

Staring at another slip of yellowed paper, Janet didn't answer.

"Earth to Janet," Kim said. "What have you found now?"

"Another note. It fell from the dress when you held it up. A dress, by the way, which will look gorgeous on you in the show, Debbie. This note is from one person only. It says, 'But still my fancy wanders free through that which might have been. Thomas Love Peacock.'"

"Wow," Debbie said. "Not the kind of note you expect to find with a wedding dress."

Kim laid the gown back in the box and smoothed the bodice. "Ladies, I think there might be yet another note." She lifted the garment out again and looked at the inside of the bodice. "A pocket. I've never seen or heard of a pocket in the bodice of a wedding dress before."

"It's over the heart," Janet said. "Is there a note in it?"

Kim pulled a folded paper from the fabric and handed it to Janet.

The cold heart of winter stole from me,
but life goes on as you shall see,
and someday, dear, in love you'll be,
and wear this dress instead of me.

"There's a story here," Kim said, "and I, for one, want to know what it is."

"It's more than a story." Janet looked at Debbie. "See if you can finish this sentence. I love a—"

Debbie grinned. "Mystery. Let's call the donor."

Janet pulled out her phone and waggled it at Kim.

"Her number's in the office," Kim said. "Let's go get it."

After tapping in the phone number, Janet held her breath and waited for Dawn Anderson to answer. She gave her friends a thumbs-up when a woman's voice said hello in her ear. "Mrs. Anderson? My name is Janet Shaw. I'm calling from Kim Smith's office in the Dennison Depot Museum. She and a friend of ours, Debbie Albright, are here too. We've been looking at the trunk you donated and wonder if you know that it has a false bottom?"

"You're joking." Dawn laughed.

"No." Janet couldn't help grinning.

"Is there anything in it?"

"Another dress," Janet said. "A special dress."

"Unless it's special because it has pockets and the pockets are stuffed with twenty-dollar bills, I'm not interested in more clothes. Make that hundred-dollar bills. A twenty doesn't go far these days."

"Sorry." Janet laughed. "There is a pocket, a *hidden* pocket, but no money. Next time you're in town, why don't you come see it?"

"I'm in Dennison now and will be for a couple more days. But is it really worth my time?"

"I tell you what," Janet said, looking at Debbie and Kim. "Debbie and I run the Whistle Stop Café here at the depot. Come for lunch tomorrow, our treat, and see what you think. How does twelve thirty sound?" Debbie gave Janet a thumbs-up.

"Might as well," Dawn said. "They say free food tastes better, don't they? I'll let you know if it's true."

"Wonderful. See you tomorrow."

When Janet disconnected, Debbie asked, "What's that look on your face?"

"Confusion," Janet said. "I can't tell if Dawn is a kidder or unusually candid." She repeated Dawn's remarks about hundred-dollar bills and free food.

"You should have told her it's a wedding dress," Debbie said. "And about the secret message *in* the pocket. Why were you so cagey?"

"I think I got rattled," Janet said. "It's silly of me, but there was something oddly familiar in her voice. And it made me want to be cautious."

CHAPTER TWO

Monday morning, bundled against the frigid, predawn cold, Janet fumbled with her key at the café's back door. Puffy quilted mittens, while toasty warm, did nothing for her fine motor skills. With her third fumble the key turned, and she let herself into the kitchen.

She shed her mittens, hat, scarf, and coat, stowed her purse, and said a prayer of thanks. Thanks for bringing Debbie home from the corporate world in Columbus with her brainstorm for the two of them to own and run this café, thanks for the ability to create the baked goods customers couldn't get enough of, and thanks for this spotless, cozy kitchen in which to practice that skill. After years of working in other people's bakeries, owning the café with Debbie was a dream come true.

The two best friends had worked out a compatible schedule for running the café. Janet arrived before dawn each morning to get the day's baking underway—scones, muffins, and cookies for the most part. Then she'd move on to eggs and bacon and other breakfast items when the café opened. They did a decent lunch trade too, so on a frosty January day like this they would offer steaming bowls of soup and hot sandwiches.

Janet slipped one of their railroad-themed aprons over her head. The apron provided full front coverage but would allow customers to see the graphic on the back of her T-shirt. Today's shirt, a Christmas present from Tiffany, her college-aged daughter, featured two perky birds pecking at a scone. Below them it said: FEED TWO BIRDS WITH ONE SCONE.

With a bounce in her step, Janet set out her recipes, ingredients, and the tools of her trade. On the menu this morning— plain scones, blueberry scones, and, for those not afraid to indulge, white chocolate peppermint scones. For anyone still following a New Year's resolution to eat healthier, she would make bran muffins with raisins.

While the first batches baked, Janet took a moment to read her devotional for the day. *The chance to be kind is always there for you,* she read. *Spreading kindness and joy is like spreading sunshine.* Janet thought of the kind people she knew and had known and how being with them warmed her. Good words to remember, especially in the depths of winter.

A couple of hours later, Debbie arrived stamping cold feet and calling good morning. She disappeared into the small office to put away her personal belongings. When Debbie returned, Janet saw her lift her nose as if to catch the aromas wafting toward her.

"What do you smell this morning?" Janet asked.

"Ahh," Debbie said, after filling her lungs on a deep inhale. "I smell a beautiful day." She chose an apron and washed her hands. "And now I'll go make sure we're ready for everyone else to share it with us when they walk through our doors."

In return for Janet's early hours and kitchen duties, Debbie handled the café's opening and closing routines. She also ordered supplies and ingredients, and often did the shopping too. Both women worked the counter as needed, with help from their invaluable part-timer, Paulette Connor.

Janet continued her ballet of taking trays from the oven, sliding more in, and preparing yet more to wait their turn. Oven timer set, and humming to herself, she picked up a tray of pastries ready for the bakery case and pushed through the swinging door into the dining room.

The morning sun shone through the café's large windows, making the yellow walls look lit from within. The deep red wainscotting, so like the red border on the apron they'd found in Dawn's trunk, ran around the room as a perfect accent. Janet wished the well-worn apron wasn't too fragile to wear, but she couldn't risk it.

Kim arrived shortly after noon and sat on a stool at the long counter. The museum was closed on Mondays, so she had time to spare before their meeting with Dawn. She perused the chalkboard behind the counter for the day's menu.

"What would you like?" Janet asked. "The chowder's thick and creamy."

"The vegetable dumpling soup is good too," Debbie said.

Paulette, on her way past with a tray of lunch orders, chimed in. "And there's nothing better than a corn muffin with a bowl of either."

"Thanks," Kim said. "Now I have the problem of making up my mind. But I'll wait until Dawn gets here to do it."

"What can you tell us about Dawn?" Janet asked.

"Not a lot."

"Because of something like doctor-patient confidentiality?" Debbie asked.

"You mean museum director-donor confidentiality?" Kim smiled. "There's some of that involved. But it's mostly that she only stuck around long enough to give me the bare minimum of information about the trunk. If the TV people disappointed her when they didn't think much of it or its lovely contents, she did a good job of hiding it. As for Janet's question yesterday, whether Dawn's candid or a kidder, that's an open question. And now you can answer it yourselves." Kim waved at a blond woman in a brown parka who'd just stepped inside.

Dawn Anderson acknowledged Kim with a nod. She moved aside so two couples could leave. Before approaching the counter, she let her gaze glance off the other patrons and the historic photos on the walls, then to the tin ceiling high above, and finally to the long planks of the original wood floor beautifully darkened with age.

Janet felt a twinge of disappointment that Dawn's survey of the café hadn't come with one of the smiles that she and Debbie were used to getting from first-time customers. But no matter, she thought, and she smiled and waved when Dawn turned to the counter. Janet did a mental double take. Not only had Dawn's voice sounded familiar, she *looked* familiar. Who was she?

Kim introduced Dawn to Janet and Debbie then indicated the chalkboard menu. By the time Kim and Dawn had decided on the clam chowder and corn muffins, several more people waited in line behind them to place orders.

"Paulette and I can handle this," Debbie said to Janet. "You go ahead with Kim and Dawn and fill me in later."

Janet assembled a tray with bowls of chowder, packets of oyster crackers, and warm muffins with butter and carried it to the table where Kim and Dawn sat near one of the front windows. Paulette followed with water glasses and three cups of coffee.

"So you think this dress with its empty pocket is something exciting." Dawn blew on a spoonful of chowder, looking from Kim to Janet through the rising steam.

"We do," Janet said. "The pocket doesn't have money in it, but I didn't say it was empty." She set her spoon down. "Dawn, have we met before? Your voice and your face... oh my goodness! Are you Dawn Draper?"

"Used to be."

"And you lived in Dennison and babysat me when I was five or six. I was Janet Hill back then."

"Oh yeah. Huh. We moved away at the end of that school year, and to tell the truth, I never liked babysitting. You were a cute kid, though. Never any trouble. But back to the dress and the pocket that isn't empty. What's so special?" Dawn looked from Janet to Kim and ate a spoonful of chowder.

"It's a wedding dress," Kim said. "Someone stitched a pocket into the bodice and left a note there. It's very sweet. You're welcome to change your mind when you see it."

Dawn, spoon halfway to her mouth, stopped. "Change my mind about what?"

"Giving the trunk to the museum," Kim said.

With a look of condescending patience, Dawn returned the spoon to her bowl. She picked a tiny muffin crumb off her plate and held it between her thumb and forefinger. "Sorry to disappoint you," she said, bringing the crumb close to her eye and squinting. "But even this crumb is bigger than whatever smidge of enthusiasm I ever had for sorting through and disposing of other people's possessions."

"But if you do—" Kim started to say.

"Really not likely," Dawn said.

Dawn looked immovable, and Kim looked bewildered. Janet decided to change the subject. Slightly. "Where did you find the trunk?" she asked. "Since I was a kid, my secret wish has been to find a trunk like that in an attic."

"A trunk full of musty old clothes?" Dawn asked.

"They're in remarkably good condition," Kim said mildly.

"They do say that one woman's trunk of junk is another woman's treasure," Dawn said. "You'll be happy to know that I did find this one in the attic. Not until after I cleared some of the other 'treasures' out of the way—dusty furniture with too many drawers full of handkerchiefs and doilies, an impressive number of warped tennis rackets and deflated basketballs, and stacks of old magazines. Stacks and stacks and *stacks* of old magazines." Dawn shook her head as though she still couldn't believe how many stacks. "After I'd cleared enough stuff that I could actually see the attic walls, I spotted the little door."

"A little door!" Janet said. "That's always been my second secret wish."

"Mine too," Kim said. She and Janet grinned at each other.

"I wasn't sure this one was real," Dawn said. "Aunt Nellie had someone paint a few of those tromp whatevers… optical illusions around the house."

"Trompe l'oeil?" Kim said. "How fun is that? I wonder who she got to do it."

Dawn finished her chowder. "Maybe Aunt Nellie did it herself. Anyway, the door in the attic turned out to be real. It leads to a crawl space built under the eaves. One more space full of stuff. A very awkward space, at that."

Janet's mind had started racing when she heard the name Nellie. She'd only ever heard of one Nellie in Dennison—Nellie Lightwood, who had died in the early fall at age eighty-four. Three or four years before she'd retired, Nellie had been Janet and Debbie's high school English teacher. Probably Kim's too. Nellie Lightwood had been a fixture at the high school for decades. "Was Nellie Lightwood your aunt?"

"By marriage," Dawn said. "My mother-in-law's sister. My children and I are her last surviving relatives."

"The end of an era," Janet said.

Dawn bowed her head and pushed muffin crumbs around on her plate. Janet resisted the urge to reach out and put her hand on Dawn's, to comfort or commiserate. Dawn didn't seem the type who would appreciate that kind of sympathy.

Kim sat forward. "Do you think the trunk and the clothes were Nellie's personal possessions? Or family heirlooms?"

"Every single last knickknack in the house, every book, chipped teacup, knitting needle, and dried-up paint brush was part of Nellie's hoard of personal possessions." Dawn pushed her empty soup bowl away.

"But—" Kim started to say.

"But I know what you mean," Dawn said. "And I'll admit it hasn't been easy figuring out what belonged to Nellie or the Lightwood family before Nellie started her crusade to bring home every bit of stray stuff that caught her eye."

Paulette stopped by the table to top off their coffee cups. "May I bring you anything else?"

"Another corn muffin?" Dawn asked.

"Aren't they delish?" Paulette said. "Be right back with one for now and one to go."

Paulette's offer brought the first real smile to Dawn's face that Janet had seen. The smile lingered until Dawn looked at Janet and Kim and asked if either of them had ever dropped in to see Nellie. They shook their heads, Janet feeling a stab of guilt. But she'd never had a dropping-by kind of relationship with Miss Lightwood.

"Don't worry about it," Dawn said. "My husband and I rarely came to see her either. So now, let me tell you about Nellie and her house."

"And her stuff?" Kim asked.

"*So* much stuff. I've been working at it steadily for three or four months, spending long weekends here."

Paulette returned with a white bakery bag and a muffin on a plate. She set them down in front of Dawn.

"Thanks." Dawn broke off a piece of the muffin and popped it in her mouth with another genuine smile. As she swallowed, she seemed to swallow the smile too, until she looked just plain tired. "Some of the weekends feel *very* long."

"It's a lot of work for one person," Janet said. "Are your children able to help?"

Dawn dismissed the question with a shrug and hand flap. "Busy jobs. Busy grandchildren. Busy in general."

"That's too bad."

"It isn't bad or good," Dawn said. "It's life. And before you ask, no, hiring someone to help won't make sense until I'm sure I've separated Nellie's eccentricities from family mementos."

"It *is* a lot to take on," Janet said. "How far do you have to travel to get here?"

"From southwest of Columbus where my family moved. Yellow Springs. It takes about two and a half hours. I never knew Aunt Nellie well, but over, say, the past decade, she seemed to get more eccentric every year. I wouldn't call her a bona fide hoarder, but she loved yard sales, and she became a collector. An eclectic collector— bringing home some of this, a lot of that, and quite a bit of the other thing too, including the kind of things you find in box marked 'free' at the end of a driveway when a yard sale is over."

"What did she do with all of it?" Kim asked.

"The few times my husband and I did come to see her, Nellie had to move boxes of misfit stuff off chairs or the sofa so we could sit. Once I found a garden trellis in the bathtub. Hanging from it were a birdhouse, minus its roof, a half-embroidered Christmas stocking, and a puppet missing its arms and nose." Dawn shook her head as if trying to dislodge that image from her head. "It didn't stay in the bathtub, though. Things seemed to move around and come and go. That's why I say she wasn't a true hoarder. The house was always clean, just…overly full. Some people rescue animals. Nellie rescued stuff. Nicked, chipped, moth-eaten, and *incomplete* stuff. That's why the trunk and the clothes surprised me."

"Like a museum and its collection policy," Kim said. "The trunk and clothes don't fit Nellie's collection policy?"

"Exactly." Dawn raised her coffee cup to Kim in salute.

"So you don't think the trunk and clothes are family heirlooms?" Janet asked.

"Nellie was probably a little girl in the 1940s," Kim speculated. "Unless her sister was much older, the clothes could have been their mother's, couldn't they?"

"Or another female relative's?" Janet asked.

"Their mother, Grammy Lightwood, was the shortest woman I've ever met," Dawn said. "No way those clothes fit her, and I never heard of cousins or aunts or other female relatives who would have been the right age to wear them in the 1940s. No, from the way the trunk was squirreled away in that crawl space, I think Nellie picked it up early on, before—maybe *years* before—the real eccentricity set in. Before she turned the house into a paradise of garage sale cast-offs. So. Now." Dawn gave them a skeptical look. "Tell me about this dress that I and the so-called experts from *Days of Yesteryear* missed and you managed to find."

As Kim told her about the wedding dress, describing it and the hidden pocket with its note, Janet watched Dawn. This woman did not impress easily.

"Huh," Dawn said when Kim's voice trailed off.

"Did you find the other notes in the trunk?" Janet asked. "They were tucked into one of the trunk's side pockets."

"I saw them and didn't think much of them. The apron I almost tossed. It didn't look like anything anyone would want, but it was wrapped around the recipe box so I put it back the way I found it."

"The quilt blocks?" Kim asked.

"I'm not into quilting."

Janet felt like echoing Dawn's "huh" but didn't want to be rude.

"Would you like to see the dress?" Kim asked. "The museum is closed to the public today, but I'll be glad to take you in."

"That's not necessary," Dawn said. "Not that I haven't got a few romantic bones in my body, but it sounds like just one more stray thing Nellie brought home. If she even knew the dress was there." She sat back and closed her eyes. "I will be so glad when the house is empty. My husband and I went through this with his mother's house. He brought way too much stuff back to our house. None of it is anything the kids are interested in, and I'm not either. The clutter. The dust. Since he died, I made some headway clearing it out. Then Nellie died. It's defeating."

This time Janet did put her hand on Dawn's.

"Well." Dawn opened her eyes and pulled her hand away. "Thanks for lunch, and sorry about raining on your wedding dress parade. I'm sure you get lots of folks trying to load the museum down with leftovers from estate sales."

"That's why museums have collection policies," Kim said. "If we weren't careful, we'd become the community's attic. But then again if no one saves everyday stuff, including letters and diaries and photographs, history loses out."

"I guess I have a collection policy too," Dawn said. "I found shoeboxes full of letters my mother-in-law wrote to Nellie starting from when my mother-in-law married and moved to Yellow Springs. I read a few of them, but who has the time? Or, to be frank, the interest. But recycling or putting them in the garbage for random people to find didn't seem right."

"Do you still have them?" Kim asked. "Or any letters Nellie wrote to your mother-in-law?"

Dawn shook her head. "Sorry. Shredding them all made the most sense. Why? You don't think you'd have found something in them about the wedding dress, do you?"

"Maybe," Kim said. "If the dress has a connection to the family."

But now we'll never know, Janet thought sadly. "Is there quite a lot left to do at the house?" she asked.

"I keep thinking I'm almost to the finish line, that I've found every possible nook and every over-crammed cranny. But there's always one more cupboard or closet I overlooked or find out is worse than I thought. It's tempting, so tempting to just shovel it all into a dumpster. And then I find an uncashed check she'd used as a bookmark. I can't, in good conscience, dump anything without looking through it, or at it, or—" She stifled a yawn.

"I can understand not wanting to hire someone to come in like a whirlwind to empty the place," Janet said, "but what about someone to help when you're there? Under your supervision?"

"Are you volunteering to come over and help this afternoon?" Dawn asked.

"I can't this afternoon but—"

"But," Dawn said, cutting Janet off and making the word sound like a door slam. This woman was clearly overwhelmed and exhausted. If Janet were in Dawn's shoes, she'd probably be prickly too.

"I only meant to say that the café doesn't close until two," Janet said, "and after that I have an appointment. I'll be happy to lend a hand this evening, though, or tomorrow after two."

"Don't worry about it. But I do appreciate the offer, and the lunch." Dawn stood to go. "I probably won't do anything more today anyway. To tell you the truth, I'm a little weirded out." She looked around the café then sat again and asked in a whisper, "What are the police like in Dennison? Can they be trusted?"

CHAPTER THREE

You can trust the Dennison police with complete confidence," Janet said without hesitation. She paused to gauge Dawn's response. Dawn didn't look immediately relieved.

Kim, her voice lowered, jumped into the silence with the question foremost in Janet's thoughts. "Do you mind if I ask why you want to know if you can trust them?"

"Isn't it interesting how bad memories stick around longer than good ones?" Dawn asked. "I had a bad experience with the police once. Nothing to do with Dennison. Something that happened years ago that I should have forgotten by now."

"Maybe a good experience will push the bad memories out of the way," Janet said.

Dawn seemed to think that over and then said, "Anything's possible."

"And something's happened now?" Kim said. "What is it?"

"Someone's been in Nellie's house. I'm pretty sure. Last night or early this morning."

"Pretty sure or sure?" Kim asked.

"Sure," Dawn said.

"But you haven't called the police," Janet said.

"No." Dawn crossed her arms over her chest.

Recognizing a classic self-protective pose, Janet checked the time and made a quick decision. "I can go with you to the police station if that will help. Or back to Nellie's house, and we can call them from there."

"I thought you were busy this afternoon." Dawn's arms tightened.

"I'll see if Paulette can stay longer today. My appointment's at three thirty. There's time. Let me help."

"I..." Dawn looked at the table then raised her eyes to Janet. "I'd appreciate that."

"I'm happy to do it. Besides, I have an in with the police," Janet said. "My husband is the chief."

Janet drove Dawn the few blocks to the redbrick Village Hall that housed the mayor's and other town offices in addition to the fire and police departments. Dawn said little on the short drive. Janet hoped she wasn't having second thoughts or feeling pushed into this, but she really did need to make the report. They parked and got out, and Dawn hesitated, looking up at the two and a half stories. "Hardly unnerving at all," Dawn said. "Come on. Might as well get this over with."

Janet had sent Ian a text before they left the café, checking to see if he was available to hear Dawn's story. Any of his officers would have been just as capable if he hadn't been free, but Janet thought the skittish woman would benefit from Ian's steady, serious attention. *In fact, he's as solid as the building and not unnerving at all.* His office door was open, so she knocked lightly on the frame. With a warm smile, Ian stood and came from behind his desk to welcome them.

"Thanks for seeing us on such short notice," Janet said.

"Always happy to when I can."

"Dawn, this is my husband, Chief of Police Ian Shaw. Ian, this is Dawn Anderson. She's Nellie Lightwood's niece, and she babysat for me when I was five or six."

"I liked the money I made more than the babysitting." Dawn shook Ian's offered hand. "And I'm Nellie's niece-in-law."

"A relation all the same," Ian said. "I'm sorry for your loss. Have a seat, and tell me what's on your mind." He waited until the women were settled in the chairs facing his desk then sat back down behind it, his handsome face open and friendly.

Dawn looked at Janet, who nodded encouragement.

"I didn't suspect anything," Dawn said. "Not until I was about to leave the house to meet Janet at the café for lunch. Not *my* house. Aunt Nellie's house. I don't live here. And I'm not positive." Dawn turned red and stopped. "I'm making a mess of this."

"I like nothing better than a good mess. You're doing fine," Ian said. "Are you staying at Ms. Lightwood's house?"

"Not since I sold or donated most of the furniture. Lately when I'm in town I get a room at the motel in Uhrichsville."

"That's a nice one," Ian said. "You've been clearing out the old place?"

Dawn launched into a description of her long-running project to empty the house, warming to her subject with Ian's attention. Janet appreciated his focus and patience. She listened to Dawn's story again, interested to see if she'd hear any new tidbits about

Nellie's collecting habits, but Dawn didn't stray into that much detail.

"So then when it was time to meet Janet and the others at the Whistle Stop," Dawn said, "I washed my hands at the kitchen sink and put on my jacket. I headed for the back door, and that's when I saw the footprints on the linoleum. They led from the back door into the kitchen. They petered out, not far from the door, the way footprints do when someone tracks something in. There weren't many prints, and they weren't mine. But I'm telling you, seeing them made my heart stop." She'd been looking at the floor as though seeing the footprints but looked up, now, with a hand to her chest. "That's a silly thing to say, isn't it? It just *felt* like my heart stopped."

"Understandable," Ian said. "Any idea what the intruder tracked in?"

"No," Dawn said, drawing out the word as if remembering. "I didn't touch them. I didn't want to bend over and get close to them. That's another silly thing. But it wasn't mud. At least not clumpy mud."

"Color?" Ian asked.

"Oh. I do know that. Black. And then I smelled something."

"What did you smell?" Ian asked.

"Nothing huge. It wasn't a big odor like a gas leak or old garbage. I would have noticed something like that while I washed my hands. I think. The thing is, I smelled it and then I didn't."

"A whiff?" Janet asked. "There and gone?"

Dawn nodded, her nose wrinkled. "It was kind of nice. Delicate. Might have been floral. Before you ask, I haven't smelled it any other day that I've been in the house over the past few months."

"A fleeting scent and footprints," Ian said. "Ms. Anderson, I'm hooked. If you're up for it, will you show me?"

"Is it all right if I come along?" Janet asked.

"Fine with me," Dawn said with a shrug.

"Do you have the time?" Ian asked.

"Debbie and Paulette have the café covered," Janet said. "We're in my car."

"Then let's get going, shall we?" Ian got to his feet. "I'll follow you."

Dawn directed Janet onto North Second Street, heading away from downtown. "It's another few blocks. On the left before you cross Blain. You can pull in around back."

"If you don't mind a short walk, I'll park on the street a few houses away in case Ian wants to look for footprints or tire tracks in the drive and surrounding area."

"Good luck with that. I drove in and backed out already today."

Janet pulled to the curb anyway, and Ian pulled in behind them.

"The Victorian on the corner," Dawn said when Ian joined them on the sidewalk.

"Is it?" Ian said. "We've been past it a thousand times, if not a hundred thousand."

"And never knew it was Nellie Lightwood's," Janet said. "I've always admired it."

"Needs painting." Dawn started down the sidewalk toward the house. "I always go in through the kitchen."

"Then let's go in through the front door," Ian said. "You can show me the footprints, and I'll take it from there."

"I ran out through the kitchen door too, when I left. I told you I didn't touch the footprints, but I might have run right over them to get out the door."

"Not a problem," Ian said.

Dawn led the way up the front steps and across the deep porch. "My mother-in-law and Aunt Nellie grew up in this house. Nellie moved back after their parents passed."

"It's a beautiful front door," Janet said. "The etched glass is gorgeous."

"Single pane. Bleeds the heat straight through it." Dawn unlocked the door and swung it open. "Lucky their parents didn't have sports-minded daughters. They'd have had softballs going straight through that window."

Janet and Ian followed Dawn into a spacious entry with a parquet floor. A wide, dark oak staircase climbed the wall to their right. The staircase turned the corner on its way to the second floor. Light coming through a tall stained glass window, which depicted a vine laden with bunches of grapes, bathed the banister and the corner landing in shades of amber, green, and purple.

Through open pocket doors, to their left, Janet saw what must have been the living room. It lay empty now, except for half a dozen sealed cardboard boxes and twice as many stuffed trash bags. A fireplace with a heavy oak mantel stood at an angle in one corner of the room. Green glazed tiles, each with a grape bunch in relief, surrounded the fireplace.

"Do you have pictures of the house from before—"

"Before the great clearance?" Dawn asked. "Probably. The house has been in the family long enough. Someone must have taken pictures over the years. My husband's great-grandparents built the place. Something like that. The kitchen's this way."

Their footsteps echoed as they crossed the entry. Janet caught a glimpse of a bookshelf-lined room before they entered a huge dining room, which also had a fireplace surrounded by glazed tiles. These were brown and patterned with oak leaves. Stained-glass panels topped each of the dining room windows. More boxes, an assortment of table lamps, a dust mop, and a broom stood against one wall. Janet wanted to tell Dawn that she should get someone to give her a hand. *She* should give Dawn a hand.

"You two can look on from the door," Ian said. "Good enough?" Janet agreed, and he looked at Dawn.

"Good enough," Dawn said. "I guess."

The women stood next to each other in the open door and watched as Ian stepped sideways then followed alongside a smudged trail leading to the outer door. He stopped in the middle of the room, nose lifted. Then Ian squatted down, took his phone from a pocket, and snapped pictures from several angles. Janet itched to go in and see the footprints from those angles for herself. Ian rose and pocketed the phone. "Ms. Anderson, you said you washed your hands at the kitchen sink before putting on your coat. Do I have that right?"

"Yes."

"What were you doing just before you washed your hands?"

"Looking at them and wondering what I'd touched that made them so grimy."

"You hadn't been dusting with a spray of some kind?" Ian asked.

"No."

"Did you pack up anything like antistatic dryer sheets?" he asked. "Or laundry detergent bottles?"

"You think the scent I smelled was on me and I didn't notice?" Dawn asked.

"Not at all. I'm trying to eliminate other possible reasons for it. Where were you working in the house today?"

"The library and the dining room."

"Listening to music or an audiobook? Wearing earbuds?"

"Look, I don't blame you for doubting me. I get it. I'm not surprised you're not taking this seriously. The thing is—"

Janet couldn't help interrupting. "Ian *is* taking you seriously."

"The thing *is*," Dawn said, "now that I'm here, I remember it more clearly."

"That's perfectly normal under stress and after a fright," Ian said. "What do you remember doing?"

"I walked to the kitchen door, right through the footprints, and it was only when I opened the door that I realized what I'd seen. So I turned around and walked back—around them that time. I looked at them. Didn't want to touch them. I listened and didn't hear anything."

"At that point did you leave?" Ian asked.

"No. I grabbed a fireplace poker out of one of the boxes and walked back through the house to see if anything was missing. Except… I didn't really walk. I sort of ran."

Visions of a muddled crime scene danced through Janet's head.

"And is there anything missing?" Ian asked.

"I don't think so, but I can't be sure."

"Will you be working here anymore today?"

"I've had enough for today."

"I don't blame you," Ian said. "I'll do a walk-through to make sure no one is in the house. I'll check around outside too."

"And we just hang out here in the kitchen?" Dawn asked.

"Tell you what. In case I do flush someone out, I'd rather not worry about you being in jeopardy."

Dawn took a key from her pocket. "Lock up when you finish. We'll wait in the car."

"One last question, Ms. Anderson. Do you keep the doors locked when you're here working?"

"Yes." Dawn bit her lip. "Okay, I've forgotten a few times, but this isn't Columbus or Cincinnati. It's Dennison. Nellie called it Dreamsville."

"That's what the troops passing through during World War II called it," Janet said. "And we all forget things sometimes."

"Do you know if anyone else has a key?" Ian asked.

"I have no idea."

"Whether you do or not," he said, "I suggest getting the locks changed."

Half an hour before Janet expected Ian home for supper, she grated cheese for the flaky cheddar biscuits he liked so much. If she offered to help Dawn at Nellie Lightwood's house, would that be a kind gesture or self-serving? Nellie had been one of her favorite teachers—tough and intimidating—and Janet would love the chance to look through the books in her library. Was there anything wrong with a gesture being kind *and* self-serving?

Janet checked the stew in the slow cooker. She dipped a spoon in for a taste to check the seasoning, blowing to cool it. *Mm, just right.*

She went back to preparing the biscuits, but the oddities of the time spent with Dawn, over lunch and then at Nellie's house, kept bubbling to the surface, just like the thick broth in the stew. She knew the stew would be savory and satisfying, but the oddities weren't satisfying at all.

Why hadn't Dawn called the police as soon as she discovered the footprints, even if she'd had a bad experience with the police somewhere else years ago? Wasn't it strange that she'd come to the café to hear about the hidden dress in the trunk *knowing* she wouldn't be interested? They'd told her they hadn't found money. Then again, they'd offered her a free lunch, so maybe that wasn't strange behavior for Dawn.

Now, more than ever, Janet wanted to find out what she could about the items so carefully packed away in the trunk. And especially hidden under the false bottom. The items in the trunk didn't strike her as the kind of haphazard collection Dawn had told them about. Given the wedding dress, she might think the trunk held a trousseau, but the other clothes weren't new and the apron was *far* from new. The notes, the recipe box, and quilt blocks didn't hint at a trousseau either.

As she rolled out the biscuits, she found herself wanting to find all this out, not so much for Dawn's sake but for Nellie's. The teacher had definitely been one of the kind people in her life. Janet had asked her to write a letter of recommendation to go with her college scholarship applications. Nellie had been happy to, and whatever she'd written had helped Janet afford college. She'd thanked Nellie, of course, and no one, even in a small town, expected students to keep in close touch with former teachers. But Janet hadn't, and after hearing Dawn's description of Nellie's house and odd habits, she wondered if Nellie could have used a friend or two to check in on her later in life. To give her a hand or lend an ear. To return her kindness.

Laddie, their sharp-eared Yorkshire terrier, gave a yip and ran to the back door. Janet popped the biscuits in the oven. Laddie knew when Ian's car was still half a block away.

"Evening, Laddie," Ian said, scooping the dog into his arms. "Evening, love," he said to Janet. "As ever, you're a sight for my eyes whether they're sore or not."

"How are your eyes tonight?" She gave him a hint by brushing the backs of her fingers across the tips of her freshly trimmed hair.

He pointed a finger at her, a look of exaggerated wonder on his face. "I was just going to exclaim—what a *difference* a half inch off makes in the rare beauty that is your gorgeous hair. May I kiss the cook?"

"You certainly may, and then you may wash your hands and set the table. Supper's in five."

Over bowls of stew with fluffy, cheesy biscuits on the side, Janet asked Ian what he could tell her about the Lightwood house. "Nothing about the investigation," she said. He rightly never discussed ongoing investigations. "But a description of the rest of the house isn't out of bounds, is it? How many rooms, for instance?"

"I didn't count, but let's see—" He put his spoon down and ticked the rooms off on his fingers. "Living room, dining room, library, sunroom, kitchen, walk-in pantry, small bedroom off the kitchen presumably for a cook, four big bedrooms upstairs, each with a fireplace. Bathroom upstairs, powder room downstairs. The attic is huge, and there's a small bedroom up there too. Plus the basement which has a few rooms of its own, though it doesn't look like they've ever been finished for any use other than storage or workshops."

"Workshops. Plural. The basement sounds huge too. You stopped counting, but I've got the general idea of its size. I'm going to make another offer to help Dawn over there."

"You already offered and she said no?"

"She didn't say no, but she asked if I could help this afternoon. It sounded more like a challenge than a request. A challenge she didn't expect me to accept but wanted me to feel guilty about. Then she said she wasn't going to do anything else there today anyway."

"I hope you don't feel guilty."

"I don't."

"Maybe ask her again, if you have time to help and want to. I'm sure she could use it. You didn't see all the stuff that's left. I can't imagine tackling it on my own. *Why* is she tackling it alone?"

"It sounds like Ms. Lightwood went in for eccentric organizing in addition to eccentric collecting. Dawn feels she needs to look through all of it to make decisions."

After the dishes were done, Ian suggested she settle herself in the den and he'd bring in cocoa. Janet did as he said, plopping onto the sofa and putting her feet up with a sigh. Their old gray cat, Ranger, saw his opportunity and came to curl up in her lap. Ian came in with the cocoa—including marshmallows—and squeezed into his recliner beside Laddie. Their dog looked at Ian hopefully.

"No cocoa for you," Ian said. "Or marshmallows."

"Did you have Ms. Lightwood in high school?" Janet asked.

"No, but she worked with the theater teacher, and whenever they needed Scottish or other British accents for a play Ms. Lightwood got

Mum or Dad to coach the actors." Ian's family had emigrated from Scotland when he was a child. He'd been young enough that he'd retained very little of his native accent, but it showed up in a word or two occasionally, tickling their college-aged daughter when it did.

"I'd forgotten she worked with the theater teacher."

"Prop manager, I think," Ian said. "Maybe the theater teacher considered accents another form of prop."

"It's funny to think of her as Nellie, isn't it? She was a good teacher. I knew that even at the time, but some of my memories of her class are uncomfortable."

"How so?"

"She was tough, and I never felt that I lived up to her expectations. She liked giving us pieces of advice. She had a name for them. Something like…" Janet rubbed Ranger between his ears, trying to remember, until the cat's purr rumbled. "She called them 'Lightwood spotlights.' I remember this one. 'Always leave a margin for the unexpected in your plans.' That's especially good to remember when you have children."

"Or crimes to solve," Ian said.

"Or crimes to perpetrate."

"I'd rather the perpetrators not plan that carefully." Ian pointed to her cocoa mug. "Are you finished? Can I get you more?"

"It was delicious, and I'm fine. Thanks. I wonder if the scent Dawn smelled counts as the unexpected. A margin of error the perpetrator didn't plan for."

"It's the scent that intrigues me most about her intruder," Ian said. "I wish we had more to go on."

"Isn't it too bad you can't take pictures of smells?"

"That's the way I feel every time you bake," he said. After a quiet moment he added, "In the end, I think Dawn was disappointed."

"With you? With your response? I don't see how she could be."

"With herself as much as anything. With how she reacted to the intruder."

"Because it scared her?"

"I'm not entirely sure," Ian said. "But she ran through the house with the poker, and she didn't immediately report it to the police. She's tackling the job of clearing the house on her own, and maybe she wanted to handle this on her own too. I have to wonder why."

CHAPTER FOUR

Debbie blew in through the kitchen door the next morning already talking. "You have a promise to keep."

"My promise not to burn the muffins? Done. Now let me get these pans out of the oven while you hang up your coat and catch your breath."

"Whatever muffins you're making, they smell divine," Debbie said as she went into their office.

"Two kinds. Oat and banana toffee," Janet said to Debbie's retreating back. "Ian's mom calls that banoffee. Think of them as unassuming banana muffins hiding swirls of delectable soft toffee."

"If there's toffee swirling, then I'm swooning," Debbie called.

The oven timer went off. Janet took two pans of the banana toffee muffins from the oven, slid two more in, and reset the timer. When she turned back to the worktable, Debbie was sitting on a stool across from her looking like an eager student.

"Kim dashed out right after you did yesterday," Debbie said. "First, give me a report on the lunch with Dawn. And after that I want your junior police chief report from the visit to the station."

"When you were a kid, did you ever have a babysitter named Dawn Draper?"

Debbie shook her head. "But you did? And she was this Dawn?"

"It is. That's why her voice sounded familiar when I called her from the museum. Maybe it was just the vague memory trying to surface that made me feel cautious, not Dawn herself."

"Makes sense," Debbie said. "So how did Dawn react when you told her about the wedding dress and the note hidden in its secret pocket? I thought I'd hear a squeal of delight."

Janet considered for a moment. "I don't think she's the squealing type."

"Was there at least a gasp of astonishment?"

"More of a shrug."

"How disappointing," Debbie said. "If she isn't the squealing or gasping type, what type is she?"

"Self-contained, unsentimental." Janet took oat muffins from their tins and arranged them on a tray for the bakery case. "She's matter-of-fact and kind of abrupt, but she's lost her mother-in-law, her husband, and now her aunt in recent years. What I saw as abrupt might be a mixture of post-holiday exhaustion, house-clearing exhaustion, and the exhaustion of grief."

"No one would be at their best with all of that piled on them," Debbie agreed.

"I offered to help her at the house—oh! I haven't told you about the house."

"I'll be happy to help there too, if she doesn't mind," Debbie said.

Janet turned a grateful smile on her. "It didn't work out yesterday, but I'll call her and offer again. She's sorting through absolutely everything."

"Makes sense."

"It does, although she seems to be pretty ruthless about what she keeps and what she trashes."

"There's only so much stuff a person can accumulate on top of what they've already accumulated."

"But a part of me mourns for the lost personal items."

"Like what?" Debbie asked. "We didn't know Ms. Lightwood after high school."

"Letters," Janet said. "Dawn found shoeboxes full of letters her mother-in-law wrote to Nellie—they were sisters. Dawn read a few then shredded all of them. So, no, we didn't know Nellie, but she was a great teacher, and now I feel like we missed out on getting to know her."

"By reading her sister's letters?"

"Or Nellie's letters to her sister. Is that too nosy? Anyway, Dawn shredded those letters too."

"And now a window into the past isn't just closed. It's broken and boarded up." Debbie looked at the time. "Whoa, I'd better put my skates on so we don't disappoint our adoring public."

Throughout their busy morning, Janet's mind turned over ways to find out about Nellie and her habit of bringing home what Dawn had called "stray stuff." There must be people who knew she'd done that. During a midmorning lull, as she stocked the bakery case yet again, her phone chirped with an incoming text. She pulled the phone from her apron pocket at the same time she saw Debbie pick up her own phone.

"It's Kim," Debbie said. "If you don't mind sticking around, she's inviting us to her office after we close. She wants to hear about the police report too."

"Sounds good." That way she wouldn't have to tell it twice and she could make up for being gone so long yesterday.

"And if we take along some of the banoffee muffins, I'll stop drooling for one now."

"That sounds good too," Janet said with a laugh. "I'll put some aside."

That afternoon, Janet knocked on Kim's office door. When Kim opened it, Janet held up a bakery bag. "We come bearing gifts." Debbie held up a drink carrier with three cups of coffee.

"You treat me too well," Kim said. "Mind you, I'm not complaining. More like bragging. Come on in."

Kim moved papers and a file aside to make room on her desk. Janet laid out three napkins and set a muffin on each. Debbie distributed the coffee cups then didn't wait to sit down before taking a bite of her muffin.

"You like?" Janet asked.

Debbie closed her eyes and only said, "Mm-hmm."

"She's been waiting all day to try one," Janet explained to Kim.

"Then say no more." Kim bit into her own muffin, and her eyes widened.

"Right?" Debbie said. "That taste sensation is banana swirled with toffee, or as Ian's mom calls it, banoffee, according to Janet. I think we should start calling them that at the café too."

Janet got a kick out of watching her friends enjoy their muffins then surprised them by setting out one more for each. They ate more slowly this time, and she finally ate hers. "My concern with calling them banoffee," she said after disposing of her napkin in the empty bakery bag, "is that people might think the 'offee' part is coffee."

"How are you able to make such good sense after eating one?" Debbie asked. "My mind turned to mush. But you're right, so banana toffee it is. Now, police report time?"

"First a question for Kim," Janet said. "If you had to choose one word to describe Dawn, what would it be? I told Debbie my impressions of her, but I'd love to know what vibe you got."

Kim sat back, sipped her coffee, and thought. "I don't know if this describes how she always is, but it's what I got off her yesterday. The word is brittle. It made me worry about her and hope she's okay. Does that make sense?"

Janet nodded slowly. "It does. I wouldn't have thought of brittle but, now that you've said the word, I think it fits. I agree with your worry too. I hope she doesn't break."

Debbie put a hand on Janet's arm. "If we can get her to let us help with the house, maybe that will help her in other ways too."

"It might at that. Now, the police station, the break-in, and the house. But not in that order, because the house!" Janet described everything she'd seen, from the front door, to the stained glass, to the barely glimpsed library, to the dining room. "I'd tell you about the kitchen too, because you know I'm all about kitchens, but that's where Dawn saw the footprints—"

"Footprints!" Debbie and Kim both exclaimed.

"That's how I felt too," Janet said. "Ian didn't allow us past the doorway to the kitchen, so we wouldn't contaminate the scene any more than it already was. Watching him, with my mind racing with all kinds of questions and possibilities, put the idea of studying the kitchen right out of my head."

Janet told them what she'd heard from Ian about the rest of the house. Debbie and Kim were suitably impressed. Even so, her description of the break-in, especially the scent, piqued their interest even more. "Bottom line," Janet said, "is that the break-in might have been nothing more than a walk-in. Dawn doesn't always lock the door when she's working at the house."

"That's understandable," Kim said. "This is Dennison after all."

"And the person didn't call out when they came inside?" Debbie asked.

"Maybe they did and Dawn didn't hear," Kim said. "If she'd been in the big basement or attic, she might not have."

"She told Ian she'd been working in the library and dining room. The dining room is right next to the kitchen and the library not far down the hall. Oh."

"What?" Debbie asked.

"Ian asked her if she'd had earbuds in. She didn't answer. Instead she got prickly and said she knew he wouldn't take her report seriously."

"Prickly or brittle," Kim said, "do *we* take her report seriously? *Was* there a break-in?"

"The professional guy believes it," Janet said.

"From all we've heard, *she* believes it," Debbie said. "Besides, what would she get out of reporting a break-in that didn't happen?"

"Hear me out," Kim said. "And this is totally hypothetical. What if the intruder was real but the intrusion was staged? What if Dawn is working with someone else?"

"To what end?" Debbie asked.

"To lay the groundwork," Kim said. "To make it believable when someone *does* break in and hauls off who knows how many valuable things still in the house?"

"Someone who smelled good," Debbie said, "but only the first time."

"Because the second time they won't wear scent or leave convenient footprints."

"Whoa, whoa." Janet was beginning to feel sick. Could they be right? Surely not. "Let's back up. Dawn inherited the house and everything in it. She owns all of it. She doesn't need to stage a break-in to steal her own property."

"Unless she can get more from insurance than from going to the trouble of selling choice bits. But you're right, Janet," Kim said. "My theory was hypothetical to begin with and now it sounds like an unlikely plot for a mystery story."

"I don't think Dawn is a good enough actor to pull that off, anyway," Janet said. "And don't you think we're being uncharitable toward someone we don't know? Let's get to know her better. Keep open minds before we allow our suspicions to get the better of us and close our hearts. I'll give her a call and set a firm date for giving her a hand."

"You have her number, right?" Debbie asked. "Why not call her now?"

"Good idea," Janet said. "Or as Dawn would say, might as well get it over with." She took her phone out and pressed Dawn's number. The phone rang and rang, and she was starting to plan what she'd say in a voice message when Dawn finally answered.

"Janet. Hi. I'm still not interested in the wedding dress."

"This isn't about the dress or anything else in the trunk," Janet said. "Debbie and I would like to give you a hand at the house. Any afternoon this week."

"I'm heading back to Yellow Springs this afternoon," Dawn said. "How does Friday grab you?"

"Debbie's right here. I'll ask her if Friday works." Janet looked at Debbie, who nodded. "Friday grabs us fine, Dawn. We close at three that afternoon, so we'll hustle with the cleanup and see you about three thirty."

"I thought you closed at two."

"Except for Fridays and Saturdays."

"Well, it is what it is," Dawn said. "So what do you make of the footprints?"

"Creepy," Janet said. "You were brave to go back through the house after you saw them. I'm more of a chicken."

"You can afford to be. You have your police chief husband to protect you."

Yes and no, Janet thought. She and Ian weren't joined at the hip. But there was no point in correcting Dawn. "I'd love to know what the intruder tracked into the kitchen. From the doorway I couldn't really tell there *were* footprints. I'm guessing you're right, though, and it wasn't mud. Not on a frigid day like yesterday, after a whole string of frigid days."

"Your chief didn't tell you?"

"Ian? No. He doesn't discuss ongoing investigations with me or anyone not involved in them."

"I'm glad to hear that," Dawn said. "But would you like to know what he told *me*?"

"If you're willing to tell me, definitely."

Dawn chuckled. "Thought you might. Why don't I tell you when you're here Friday."

"Great. We'll see you then."

Dawn disconnected with another chuckle.

Janet looked at Debbie and Kim as she pocketed her phone. "Dawn has information about the footprints. But she's making us wait until we're there to tell us."

"What?" Debbie said. "Why wait?"

"I get the feeling she's using the promise of footprint information to make sure we show up."

"Now I wish I could go with you," Kim said.

"You can't play hooky for one afternoon?" Janet asked.

"Friday afternoon? So tempting," Kim said. "But I better not. Someone has a fashion show to plan."

"Kim!" Janet said. "We're leaving you in the lurch."

"Don't you worry." Kim waved her off with a laugh. "I'll get plenty of work out of you before the show."

"Give us marching orders whenever you're ready," Debbie said. "But isn't it amazing? January can be such a cold, slow-as-molasses month, and suddenly here we are with the show plus two mysteries to warm the cockles of our hearts—the mystery of the break-in, and the mystery of the hidden wedding dress. I mean, who hides a wedding dress?"

"Who adds a pocket inside the bodice of a wedding dress and leaves an enigmatic note in it?" Janet asked.

"I have to say, the mystery behind the wedding dress brings out the romantic in me," Kim said. "I'd love to solve it in time to tell the story during the fashion show. It'll add just the right touch."

"Then let's leave the break-in to Ian and his buddies in blue and concentrate on the wedding dress," Janet said. "Can we see it again?"

Kim took them to the workroom and unlocked the door. Janet and Debbie oohed and aahed when they saw the clothes from the trunk on padded hangers arranged on one of the museum's long, mobile coatracks.

"It's like the dresses are waiting for someone to come home," Janet said. "But are there enough for a fashion show?"

"We'll make it work," Kim said. "I have a few ideas up my sleeve and volunteers working on them."

Debbie had made a beeline for the wedding dress and looked in the pocket. "Kim? The note?"

"Over here." Kim crossed to a worktable. "Anything from the trunk that can't hang, including the notes, is here. A volunteer photographed everything—quilt blocks, notes, recipe cards—the works."

"Can we have copies of the pictures?" Janet asked. "They'd be handy to show people what we're talking about when we start asking around about the trunk items." And it would mean easy access to the recipes on the cards! She couldn't wait.

"Call them what they are," Debbie said. "Not trunk items. Trunk *treasures*."

"Sure thing," Kim said. "I'll put them in a shared file named 'Trunk Treasures' and send you the link."

Janet took the wedding dress on its hanger from the rack and held it up to Debbie. "It truly looks like the perfect fit for you."

"That dress and its mysterious story is turning all three of us into romantics," Debbie said. "Don't you think we should find someone of a more appropriate—meaning younger—age?" She took the dress from Janet and returned it to the rack. "And do you think we'll actually be able to track down the story?"

"When in doubt," Kim said, "ask Dennison's human database."

"Your mom?" Janet asked with a chuckle. "Does she know you call her that?"

"Ray came up with it, and she's proud of it," Kim said, taking out her phone. "I'll check to see when she's free. As you know, the database is also a bit of a social butterfly." Kim's centenarian mother, Eileen Palmer, had a vast knowledge of the town she'd lived in her whole life. Ray Zink, a veteran of World War II, had lived most of his life in Dennison too.

While Kim talked to her mother, Janet looked over the recipe cards laid out on the table. Spam with scrambled eggs? Creamed chipped beef on toast? Pass. But Welsh rabbit—melty cheese sauce served on an English muffin, no meat in sight—she could get into that. And if she made the English muffins herself? Maybe they could add Welsh rabbit, or rarebit, as it was sometimes called, or one of the other wartime recipes to the Whistle Stop Café menu to help drum up interest in the vintage fashion show.

"This evening is the best time for Mom," Kim said, holding her phone to her chest. "And for me."

"Sounds like a plan," Janet said.

"Say hi to Eileen for me, and you can fill me in tomorrow," Debbie said. "Greg and I have plans."

"Nice." Janet loved how close Debbie and Greg Connor had grown since Debbie moved back to town. "You know, if Dawn is right about Nellie's collecting habits, tracking down the story behind the wedding dress really might be a lost cause. Think how long the dress might have been hidden. It's possible that neither Nellie nor the person she got the trunk from knew the dress was there."

"Let's not lose hope before we start," Debbie said.

"Oh, I'm not," Janet said. "But do you remember in English class how Nellie pushed us to dig deeper into stories?"

"Don't look at me," Kim said, joining them after saying goodbye to her mother. "Nellie sounds like a character, but she must have taught at the high school after my time."

"I remember," Debbie said. She fixed Kim with a fierce look and punctuated each of her next words with a finger jab. "You mark my words. What you see on the surface is just the beginning of understanding a story."

"If she was that passionate in front of her students, I'm not surprised you remember," Kim said. "Are you having flashbacks, Janet?"

Janet had her hands over her face but only because she was laughing so hard. Debbie had captured the pure essence of Ms. Nellie Lightwood. Bringing her laughter under control, she decided it was the perfect time to look more deeply into Nellie's own story.

CHAPTER FIVE

Today I turned twenty. To me that seems momentous, but I know it isn't really. Also momentous, to me, is that I've never had a diary or journal before. That has changed thanks to my work pal, Deanna Lightwood.

Dee is brilliant. She's a month shy of twenty-four and already the bank manager's personal secretary. More proof of her brilliance—when silk and nylon started being rationed because of the war in Europe, she jumped right on the no stockings bandwagon. She says it doesn't have to be the no fashion bandwagon, though, because she's heard of the most incandescently brilliant idea. She's right too. She's the first girl I know to draw a stocking seam up the back of her leg. She calls it the trompe l'oeil of leg fashion. She also knows that royal blue is my favorite color, and that's why I'm now writing in this royal-blue five-year diary—my birthday present from her.

I wish I could say that I will write here every day, but I know better than to make that promise. "The best laid schemes o' Mice an' Men gang aft agley." That's from Robert Burns in his poem "To a Mouse." I love his poems, I love poetry, and I love my Gran. She came to the USA from a small village called Dornie on the west coast of Scotland, and her accent and words sound just like Robert Burns when she gets angry. That isn't often. She and Grandad gave me a book of his poetry for my birthday. They don't expect me to write home every day because they know how plans can go off-kilter, or gang agley, as Gran and Burns say. I will try, though, to keep a record of the exciting highlights of my life here in Dennison, Ohio, as an ordinary bank secretary, not a bank manager's or president's secretary (and that's good enough for me).

September 4, 1941

A letter came from Gran and Grandad today. They live in Steubenville, where I grew up. Steubenville is east of here, almost at the Pennsylvania border. Grandad helped build the new Steubenville High School. They started construction in 1938 and finally finished it in January this year. It takes up a whole city block. The newspaper calls it the first million-dollar high school in Ohio. Gran is a seamstress. She can sew anything. Embroider too.

We used to live on a farm, but the depression came along and Grandad couldn't make it work. Losing the farm nearly broke Gran's and Grandad's hearts, but they never let it show. I was ten and didn't know any better than to ask why they weren't crying too. First Gran said "wheesht," her word for hush, then she hugged me to her and said they'd already cried enough tears for a lifetime. She meant when my parents died. They were in a motor car accident when I was a baby. I told Gran I would cry for her and Grandad anytime they needed more tears.

Grandad sold the farm for what he could and bought a drafty old place in town. They run it as a boardinghouse. Grandad says Gran cooks like an angel, and I agree. When they opened the boardinghouse, Gran embroidered a Bible verse to hang in the entry. It's Romans 12:12. "Rejoicing in hope; patient in tribulation; continuing instant in prayer."

My full name is Joyce MacBeath Terrell. MacBeath is Gran's maiden name. I moved here to Dennison last year, after taking a secretarial course. I work at the First National Bank, which is on Grant Street right next door to a church, and the church is right next door to Village Hall where the police station is. Dee works at the First National too, of course, and that's how we are such good friends.

I am living away from home for the first time, but I have my own room in a boardinghouse like the one Gran and Grandad run. That makes me feel closer to them. This house is run by Mrs. Bartlett. She only takes in young women. Gran's letters always have questions about how Mrs. Bartlett does things here. Gran wants to make sure Mrs. Bartlett is running a good Christian home, and she also likes hearing about things she can do better at her own boardinghouse. Gran says she likes innovation just like James Watt did. He improved the steam engine. Gran says we're related to Watt. Steam practically shoots out her ears when Grandad says if Watt was a relative at all then it was way back in the mists of time, and he was a cousin more times removed than his old shoes have been removed from his feet.

September 7, 1941

A group of friends went apple picking this afternoon in an orchard outside of town. Dee organized it and brought along her kid brother, Theo. Kid brother, my foot! He's barely two years younger than she is, and that makes him two years older than me. He has the same shiny brown hair and eyes Dee does. He's much more serious than Dee but laughs when Dee teases him about it. He graduated from Cedarville College, over near Dayton, last year. He's working in the office at the T. Lanning Department Store just down the street from the bank. Lanning's is about the tallest building in Dennison and is most certainly the nicest store.

I worried I might be melancholy going with the gang to a farm. I miss our farm every bit as much as Gran and Grandad. But on a fine day like today, with the fresh air and blue skies, I perked right up. Some of the girls looked sideways at me on account of my dungarees. But I said how do you expect to climb a ladder in a skirt? Or a tree? Maybe they hadn't planned to do any climbing. Dee said she was jealous and plans to march down to the T. Lanning Department store and ask for Mr. Theo Lightwood to sell her a pair of dungarees. She's a hoot.

I came home with a peck of apples and gave all but the one I'm eating to Mrs. Bartlett. She says she'll make apple cream pie for the boarders. She got the recipe from an Amish woman she knows in Sugarcreek, which isn't too far from here.

It's too bad we didn't go pear picking because Mrs. Bartlett likes to say that she is a Bartlett and she looks like a Bartlett. I like her rosy cheeks.

September 11, 1941

Mrs. Bartlett and some of the other boarders and I listened to President Roosevelt's Fireside Chat on the radio tonight. The girls and I had been listening to the Kraft Music Hall with Bing Crosby. Lucille Ball was his guest. They were a hoot together. We were laughing over one of their funny stories right up until Mrs. Bartlett came in and changed the channel and hushed us so she could hear the president. When we heard Mr. Roosevelt's words, we forgot all about Bing Crosby and Lucille Ball.

A Nazi submarine sank another American ship. This one, the USS Greer, was a destroyer on the way to Iceland with its American flag flying. And carrying mail! This makes four vessels sunk or attacked while flying the American flag. Mr. Roosevelt said it was piracy both legally and morally, and the time for defense is now. At the end of the chat, he talked about the inner strength of a free people, and duty, and righteousness, and how with divine help and guidance we'll stand our ground. I wish I could remember his words exactly. They made me want to stand up with my hand over my heart. Our world is changing.

CHAPTER SIX

"You're as punctual as one of our troop trains back in the day," Eileen Palmer said when Janet and Kim walked into Good Shepherd that evening. She rose from a chair in the reception area, setting a magazine neatly on a table with others. Eileen, still upright, mobile, and sharp at age 101, had been the stationmaster in Dennison during World War II. Her eyes lit up when she saw the white bakery bag in Janet's hand. "Goodies?" Eileen asked. "Did you bring plates?"

"I brought a plate for you, if you'd like a scone now," Janet said. "I brought half a dozen, and the rest are for you and your friends."

"If you want to share," Kim said.

"Even better," said Eileen. "And your box, Kim? That looks like something from the museum."

"I've always known you have X-ray vision, Mom."

"Sign in, then, and let's go to my room."

Janet and Kim greeted the receptionist at the desk and signed the visitors' register. Then they fell in beside Eileen, walking on either side of her. As they passed the library, Janet caught sight of Ray Zink.

"Hi, Ray," Janet called. He looked up from the jigsaw puzzle he was working on and waved.

"This is how I get some of my best exercise," Eileen said. "That's why I'm glad my room is nearly at the end of this hallway."

"Mom's into chair exercise too," Kim said.

"Oh, I love our sessions." Eileen pumped her arms. "I especially enjoy yoga, range of motion, and something called Zumba. I tell you, Janet, we are with it here at Good Shepherd. Well, now." Eileen stopped short, hands on her hips. "What's that hanging from my doorknob?"

Janet peered toward Eileen's door at the end of the hall. "Is it a cone?"

"Oh ho!" Eileen said with a delighted chuckle. "Come along. I know what it is."

In a few more yards, Kim identified it. "A party hat! It's hanging by the elastic."

"A New Year's party hat, to be exact," Eileen said. She covered the remaining yards to her door at a sprightly clip.

"Were you at some kind of wild Good Shepherd New Year's Eve celebration and left your hat behind?" Janet tapped the hat to make it swing from the doorknob.

"Shh. I'll tell you when we're inside." Eileen unlocked her door. "Bring the hat with you, Janet."

Janet slipped the hat from the doorknob and smiled at the photograph above Eileen's nameplate on the door. The picture showed Eileen at twenty, in her stationmaster's uniform, smiling in the open doorway of a train at the Dennison Depot. Eileen amazed Janet as a centenarian-plus-one. She would love to have known Kim's delightful, venerable mother back in the day.

"Sit down, sit down," Eileen said, lowering herself into her well-worn recliner. "Put the hat right here on the end table."

"And a scone?" Janet asked.

"I'll wait a bit for the scone. I think Ray won't be able to resist stopping in to see you, and he'll want one. On second thought, hang the hat on the inside doorknob. That way Ray won't see it with the door open."

Kim did as her mother asked, and then she and Janet sat in the two wingback chairs across from her in the cozy sitting area she'd created in her room. "What's this all about, Mom?"

"We have a prankster in the building," Eileen said with a clap of her hands. "I call her the Mad Hatter. *Her* because, as you've seen, it's mostly women here. The whole thing is simple nonsense, of course, but when you find a party hat on your doorknob, you bide your time then sneak it onto someone else's doorknob."

"So you have multiple pranksters," Janet said. "An army of Mad Hatters."

"Yes! And I don't want Ray to see the hat." Eileen's smile grew wider. "Now that I have it, I'm going to sneak it onto his doorknob. Never a dull moment at Good Shepherd."

"Never a dull moment around the depot either," Kim said. "We have a couple of new mysteries and hope you can give us clues to solve them."

"At *least* a couple," Janet said.

Eileen listened attentively as they took turns telling her about the trunk and describing the clothes, the quilt blocks, recipe box, and the two-part notes. They saved the false bottom and the wedding dress with its hidden note for last.

"Well, I'll be. I've heard that having pockets in your wedding dress is a new trend," Eileen said. "One of the women at the other end of the hall has a very fashionable great-granddaughter who wouldn't agree to any wedding dress unless it had pockets for her tissues and lipstick. So very practical. But I can't say that I've ever heard of a pocket hidden in the bodice of a wedding dress."

"It appears to have been added later," Kim said. "An afterthought."

"For that rather melancholy note. Even more interesting," Eileen said. "And you say the trunk came from the old Lightwood house? I've always heard that it's a lovely home."

"It absolutely is," Janet said. "You've never been inside?"

Eileen shook her head. "The Lightwood children, my generation of them, were ahead of me in school and you know how that goes. Like trains that pass in the night."

"Part of the mystery of the trunk is that it may have nothing at all to do with the Lightwood family," Janet said. "From what we've learned so far, Nellie Lightwood loved garage sales and estate sales."

"Janet's putting it more nicely than Dawn," Kim said. "Dawn Anderson is Nellie's late nephew's wife. She's the one tasked with clearing the house out. She hasn't come right out and said that Nellie was a packrat or hoarder, but Nellie apparently loaded the house with the stuff she brought home from the sales."

"*Stuff* is Dawn's word," Janet said. "Dawn thinks the trunk and everything in it is more of that stuff."

"But you don't think that's the case?" Eileen asked.

"We don't know enough yet to say one way or the other," Janet said.

"That's the smart way to approach a mystery." Eileen nodded her approval. "Base your theories on what you know is true and on what you learn to be true, not on what you hope. Is the wedding dress in that box?"

"No, sorry, Mom. The clothes are better off staying at the museum. But I brought the quilt blocks and recipe box, and I have pictures of the clothes on my tablet."

"Won't it be fun if I recognize the dress? Or any of the clothes? That seems unlikely, but you never know."

"You might recognize some of the names on the recipes or embroidered on the quilt blocks," Janet said. "One of the recipes is from my grandmother. My mother's mother. They lived on a farm about forty miles from here. She passed when I was seven."

"You've found a real treasure," Eileen said. "Let's take a look at those clothes, Kim."

Kim moved a hassock to sit on next to Eileen's recliner and handed her mother the tablet. "Swipe to the left to see the next picture."

Eileen swiped through the clothes, remarking on styles she remembered wearing and seeing. "These pictures do take me back," she said, "but I can't recall a specific woman wearing these items."

"Swipe one more time and you'll see the wedding dress," Kim said.

"There now, isn't that cute as a button," Eileen said.

Janet watched as Eileen's eyes took in every inch of the dress.

"Tea length was very popular at that time," Eileen said. "Even with the pleats, the whole dress used less fabric than the gowns we saw before the war. That's when the slimmed-down profile came along in women's fashion. Don't you just love the lace bodice? Are those beads across the shoulders?"

"Yes," Janet said. "It's beautiful, isn't it? The pocket is sewn inside the bodice so that it's over the heart."

"Touching," Eileen murmured, but she handed the tablet to Kim and shook her head. "I don't remember ever seeing that dress, and I did go to my fair share of weddings back then. The lace and beads and pleats are fairly distinctive. I wish I could help."

"Not to worry." Kim lifted the lid from the box. She turned the lid over and used it as a tray to hold the quilt blocks she pulled out. "These were meant to be pieced together into an autograph quilt, which I'm sure you've figured out. Each block has an embroidered signature. Look through them and see if you recognize any of the names." She put the box lid on her mother's lap.

"The fabrics...you've brought back such memories this evening." Eileen stroked the first square then traced the signature with her fingertip, and went on to the next.

"The fabrics are simple patterns," Eileen said, "made into a simple quilt design, but that time in our world wasn't simple at all. Many of these names I don't know or possibly don't remember. You saw this one, I'm sure—Thelma Lightwood?"

"Which one?" Kim took the block from her mother. "Um, no." She looked at Janet. "Thelma Lightwood."

"What? How did we miss that?"

"Chalk it up to terrible handwriting," Eileen said. "Thelma was Nellie's mother. I knew Nellie's parents, Theo and Thelma Lightwood, but not well. I remember Nellie and her younger sister even less well, and I don't remember the younger girl's name at all. Some of these other names are familiar too, but they're either no longer living or haven't lived in Dennison for years. These two, though..." Eileen held up two blocks. "Dorothy Simms and Ada

Carpenter. I haven't bumped into them in several years, but I believe they're still with us."

Janet made a note of the names on a small spiral-bound pad she pulled from her purse. "For the ones who've passed away, do you know if they have family still living in Dennison?"

"I haven't thought of most of them in years, and I might need a good night's sleep to find them up here." Eileen tapped her forehead. "If Ray comes along, we'll ask him what names he recognizes. Make him work for his scone."

"Good plan," Kim said. "We'd also like to know why the quilt was never pieced together. Any thoughts there?"

"None at all. Nor any idea who the quilt was intended for," Eileen said. "I'm sorry."

"There's absolutely nothing to be sorry about, Mom. I have one more piece of treasure to show you." Kim took the apron from the box and held it up.

"I see that and immediately smell pie," Eileen said. "Doesn't that look quaint and old-fashioned?"

"I've fallen in love with it," Janet said. "We want to find a similar fabric and make aprons like it for the café."

"Oh yes," Eileen said. "As much as I love the ones you usually wear, I would dearly love to see you wearing aprons like this one too."

"I keep saying I'll search online for reproduction fabrics," Kim said. "I'll make a note."

"Talk to Bonnie at Sticks & Threads first," Eileen said. "If she can't find it, no one can."

"I'll do that," Kim said. "Be vocal about shopping local."

"Can you imagine if people today bought flour in pretty sacks and then turned the cloth into clothes?" Janet asked.

"Somehow I don't see that happening," Kim said with a laugh.

"Knock knock," Ray Zink called from the doorway.

"Roll on in here, Ray," Eileen said. "We have a job for you, and we'll pay you in baked goods."

"I'll feel like a millionaire," Ray said.

While Ray got situated, Janet took two paper plates from her bakery bag and put a scone on each. Ray, who'd be turning ninety-nine in June, was a great favorite of hers. He had sold his old family home, a wonderful example of a Craftsman bungalow, to Debbie when she moved back to Dennison. Now he lived at Good Shepherd— and enjoyed spending time with Eileen. He also knew that when Janet or Debbie came for a visit, they usually brought baked treats from the Whistle Stop Café. Now he ate his scone, listening intently while Kim gave him a quick description of the trunk and its mysteries.

"Tell them about the intruder too." Janet smiled at Eileen's and Ray's rapt expressions as Kim started in on that part of the tale.

"I'll do what I can to help with the names," Ray said. "But after eating that buttery scone, I doubt you want my paws all over your quilt blocks or recipe cards. Why don't you read the names out? That'll save me trying to decipher some of that handwriting too."

"I like that efficiency," Kim said. "I've also got pictures of the blocks and the recipe cards I can leave with you, Mom. Looking at them again in the morning might help."

As Kim read the names, from the quilt blocks first and then the recipe cards, Janet wrote down the names Eileen and Ray recognized.

In the end, although Eileen recognized a few more than Ray, neither recognized many at all, and most of the women they did recognize no longer lived in Dennison.

"From the names we know and when they lived here," Eileen said, "I'd guess the recipes were collected in the '40s. And there's the reason Ray doesn't remember as many of the women as I do. Those war years both sped by and dragged on so much longer than any of us imagined, and he was away for a good chunk of them."

"But we finished the job we set out to do," Ray said.

Janet watched Eileen reach over and grasp Ray's hand. He patted Eileen's in return.

Something Ray had just said reminded her of Dawn. Something about unfinished business. Unfinished *projects*.

"Dawn Anderson described a lot of the things in the odd assortment of stuff Nellie Lightwood collected as incomplete," Janet said. "The quilt blocks fall into that category. You might say the recipe box does too, because there are blank cards in the back of the box. Maybe even the two-part notes. They were started by one person and finished by another."

"The notes are a stretch," Kim said. "And there's nothing unfinished about the clothes or the wedding dress."

"Except the note in the hidden pocket makes it sound like the wedding dress was never worn," Eileen said. "Isn't that an unfinished wedding?"

"I like that, Eileen," Janet said.

"Another stretch, and stretching is good for all of us." Kim started packing away the items she'd brought.

"The quilt blocks and recipe box are both full of names and handwriting," Janet said. "The notes are handwritten too. They were all together in the trunk with the dress. I can't help thinking they're connected."

"Isn't the most likely connection that everything in the trunk belonged to one person?" Kim asked. "Or was put there by one person? As for handwriting, it was everywhere back then. That's what people did. They wrote in beautiful cursive."

"A lost art, I fear," Ray said.

"They still teach it in Ohio schools, but so many other states have dropped it," Kim said. "And if kids don't learn to write cursive and read it, how will they be able to read primary source materials? Or their grandparents' letters? Sorry, I'll get off my soapbox now."

"Janet?" Eileen peered at her. "You suddenly look lost."

Janet shook her head. "Not me, just whatever connection or point I thought I was making. I might not have been explaining it well enough, but more likely it didn't make sense to begin with."

"Kim's digression derailed your train of thought." Eileen laughed. "It happens to me more and more often. Can you nudge it back on?"

"I think my train entered a tunnel without a headlight," Janet said with a laugh. "For what it's worth, Kim, I agree with you about the demise of cursive writing."

"And I think we can all agree that the person connecting the trunk treasures is Nellie Lightwood," Kim said. "We need to find out more about her. By Dawn's own admission, she hadn't known Nellie well, but is she right that Nellie never married?"

"The note in the hidden pocket hints that the dress was being saved for someone," Eileen said. "Perhaps Nellie."

"As a lifelong bachelor, I'm not able to contribute much to the wedding dress discussion," Ray said, "but try talking to your Dawn Anderson again. Find another way to ask her about Nellie rather than point-blank. She may have said they weren't close, but she might know more than she realizes."

"Ray is great at getting new residents to open up and feel at home here," Eileen said.

"That sounds like a gift," Janet said. "Debbie and I will try that when we go help Dawn at the house on Friday. We should talk to other old students of Nellie's too. Do any of you know if Nellie went to church anywhere?"

They shook their heads.

"Concerning the intruder," Ray said. "Can you find out find out if anyone besides Dawn has a key to Nellie's house? That might lead you to the culprit."

"Ian recommended new locks," Janet said.

"Good, because in my experience, a snoop will snoop again. And with those wise words, I will bid you all good night."

"Good night, Ray. Thanks." Janet collected the paper plates and napkins and disposed of them. "Thank you too, Eileen. We should be on our way."

"Good night, Mom. We'll see ourselves out."

"Nonsense." Eileen slowly raised herself from her chair. "I'll see you as far as my door. The evening's been a delight. You've given me so much to think about." At the door, she put her hand on the knob and encountered the party hat Kim had hung there. "I have my Mad

Hatter escapade to plan too. Such a busy life. Oh! That reminds me. There's another mystery that's popped up in Dennison, and it has the residents of Good Shepherd all atwitter. In fact, it might be what gave our Mad Hatter her idea."

"We're all agog, if not yet atwitter," Kim said. "What is it?"

"Some kind soul, an unknown knitter, is leaving handknitted mittens and hats around town with notes saying they're for whoever needs or wants them."

CHAPTER SEVEN

riday morning, after frying doughnuts and baking muffins and scones, Janet prepared her test batch of dream bars. First came the brown sugar shortbread bottom layer. While that baked, she whisked two eggs, dark brown sugar, vanilla, sweet flaky coconut, pecans, a bit of flour, and baking powder. She took the shortbread base from the oven, let it cool, then poured the eggy coconut mixture over it and slid it back into the oven, wishing Grandma Faye could see her. Well, maybe she could. With that comforting thought, an idea popped into Janet's head. If the bars turned out as well as she hoped, she would add them to the café menu with a new name—Grandma Faye's Dream Bars.

While the bars baked, Janet thought about all the directions their minds were suddenly going in since they'd looked through the trunk. So many intriguing mysteries, so little time. She was especially taken with the unexpected kindness of the person leaving handknitted mittens and hats around town. She wanted to know who this anonymous knitter was. Not to expose the knitter but to thank her—or him or them if there was more than one—and then maybe she could contribute something toward buying more yarn. Too bad, she mused, that leaving anonymous baked goods around town would be more likely to alarm people than charm them.

She idly doodled a sketch on the back of a shopping list she'd made for Debbie. In the center she drew a circle as a hub and then added spokes. She wrote *Nellie* in the hub then labeled the spokes: *wedding dress, other clothes, two-part notes, recipe box,* and *quilt blocks.*

Debbie arrived, calling good morning. Janet, studying the drawing, waved.

"What have you got there?" Debbie came to look over Janet's shoulder. "Hmm." Debbie took the pencil and slid the sketch away from Janet. She added a wiggly line underneath the hub and spokes and labeled the line *mystery hats and mittens.* "Now your sketch looks like the sun shining down on a landscape. Wouldn't it be a nice design for a quilt block?"

"You're a nut," Janet said, laughing, "but you're right. It would."

Debbie tied on an apron and, humming "Wait Till the Sun Shines, Nellie," went to get the dining room ready for business.

One of their first customers that morning was a favorite—Harry Franklin. He had spent his entire working life with the railroad, starting as a Dennison Depot porter at age fifteen in 1943 and going on to become a train conductor after the war ended. The station still drew him each morning, and in good weather he sat with his faithful canine companion, Crosby, watching the freight trains go by. In almost any kind of weather, he stopped at the café for a tasty, hot breakfast.

"Good morning, Harry," Janet said, sliding a cup of coffee across the counter to him. "Eggs over easy?"

"With toast and skip the bacon," he said patting his stomach. "A little bit too much holiday going on in my middle section, if you know what I mean."

"Coming right up," Debbie said. "I'll get it, Janet. You ask Harry if he knows the anonymous knitter."

"What's that you say?" Harry said.

Janet explained about the hats and mittens showing up around town and asked if he'd seen any.

"I saw a hat on the bench outside the other day," Harry said. "Didn't think anything of it. Just that some poor fellow with a cold head lost it. But this isn't the first time we've had a knitting angel."

"I like that description," Janet said. "When did it happen before? I've never heard of that in Dennison."

"Some years ago. Five? Ten?" Harry shrugged and sipped his coffee.

"Any idea who was behind it then or is now?" Janet asked.

"Someone who can knit better than I ever could."

Debbie returned with his breakfast in time to hear his remark. "I didn't know you were a knitter, Harry."

"Not so much a knitter as someone with the ability to turn any piece of yarn into a snarled knot." Harry chuckled. "At the beginning of the war, my mother tried to teach my brother and me so we could help her knit socks for the soldiers." He shook his head. "You have never seen anyone look as peeved as my mama did when she took the needles away from me again. She said she was afraid if I kept at it I'd end up hurting myself or anyone within reach. I thanked her and went out and got a job shoveling snow."

Harry's attorney granddaughter, Patricia, arrived on the gusts of Harry's laughter. She kissed her grandfather's forehead, took the stool next to him, and sighed happily over the peppermint mocha

Debbie put down in front of her. "What's got you in stitches this morning, Pop Pop?"

Patricia's warm laughter followed Harry's retelling of his story. Janet picked out a beautiful muffin and set it on a plate for her. "What prompted that tale of woe?" Patricia asked.

"Janet's searching for the elusive anonymous knitter."

"Leaving hats and mittens? I heard about that starting up again," Patricia said.

"Why did I not know about the first time years ago?" Janet asked. "Was my head stuck in a snowdrift?"

"Or a muffin tin," Debbie said. "You were up in the wee hours baking your way to glory long before we opened the café. Between working odd hours and keeping up with Tiffany, I'm not surprised it never got back to you."

"From what I heard, it wasn't just anonymous hats and mittens the first time around," Harry said. "A pretty birdhouse here, a string of bright beads there. All manner of things. Not many, mind, but often enough that you kept your eye out for the unusual."

"And I guess the police never got involved, or Ian might have said something," Janet said.

"No need for police when the intention is good wishes," Harry said.

"Turn around and let's see your T-shirt this morning, Janet," Patricia said.

She obeyed, knowing they'd see a picture of a scone dripping with jam labeled Sc-ONE, and two more scones underneath labeled Sc-TWO.

"Perfect," Janet said when Kim stopped in after the lunch rush. "It's quiet, and I now have three guinea pigs to test my very first try at Grandma Faye's Dream Bars. Are you game?"

Kim, Paulette, and Debbie immediately sat down on stools at the counter. Janet laughed and slid a plate with a treat on it to each of them. She took one for herself too.

Paulette's eyes widened with her first bite. "These," she said solemnly, "are something extra special."

Kim, eyes closed, could only nod.

"You need to add these to the list of cookies you package for sale at the museum ticket window," Debbie said.

The individual cookies they placed at the ticket window had proved to be the perfect temptation for impulse buyers. Folks loved their cookies and loved the convenience of the prepackaged dozens available in the café too.

"They are sigh-worthy, aren't they?" Janet said. "Sad to say, we can serve them at room temperature, but for storage they should be kept refrigerated because of that delicious gooey thing they've got going on. We can still put some in the bakery case and keep prepackaged dozens in the fridge." And Grandma Faye's Dream Bars were definitely going into the cookbook she was putting together too.

"Anything new, Kim?" Debbie asked.

"Only that I wish I could come with you to Dawn's this afternoon. Oh, and a suggestion," Kim said. "I thought of this after we talked to Mom and Ray. I called and gave them this suggestion too. When we talk about the wedding dress, when we're looking for information or leads or show anyone the pictures of it, let's not mention the pocket and the note."

"Why not?" Debbie asked.

"We don't know what the dress is worth," Kim said. "Possibly not much, but possibly quite a bit."

"And there are dishonest people out there," Janet said. "So we'll keep the pocket to ourselves the way Ian and his officers sometimes keep key details of a crime to themselves."

"Exactly," Kim said. "Anyone who really knows the dress should also know about the pocket."

"It might be too late for caution," Debbie said. "We told Dawn about the pocket."

"We'll ask her not to say anything," Janet said. "It'll be fine."

Janet drove them to the Lightwood house that afternoon. On the way she told Debbie about Ray's suggestion to find another way to ask Dawn about Nellie. "He says we should try to avoid asking point-blank questions."

"Worth a try," Debbie said. "Sideways questioning. Questions that come in at an oblique angle. I like that."

"You make it sound very scientific," Janet said.

"Mathematical. I liked geometry. Oh, and I do like this place," she said when Janet pulled to the curb in front of the Lightwood house. "I can picture five or six children, each one a year apart, all dressed in matching sailor suits and dresses and straw hats with ribbons down the back, marching down the front steps."

"I picture a tea party on the front porch, women in long skirts and their hair piled high, sitting in rattan chairs with plates of little sandwiches at their elbows," Janet said. "Shall we, my dear?" They linked arms, climbed the front steps, and crossed the wide porch to ring the bell.

Dawn opened the door. Dark half circles that hadn't been there on Monday rimmed her eyes. "I wasn't sure you'd show," she said. "But I'm glad you did. I appreciate it." She turned on her heel and crossed the large entryway toward the stairs.

Janet and Debbie looked at each other, shrugged, and stepped inside.

"Turn the deadbolt and come on up," Dawn called as she trudged up the long staircase. "I saved the footprints so Debbie can see them, but we'll look at them later. Work first."

They hurried after her, catching up on the landing, and followed her to a corner room. Dawn flipped a switch by the door and a light fixture in the ceiling came on. She threaded through a slalom course of packing boxes to a window and opened the blinds. Apart from a fireplace, the walls were lined with mismatched bookcases, each one packed with books.

"A second library," Janet said. "That's a serious book habit."

"An obsession," Dawn said. "Nellie rarely met a book she could pass up, and once a book was hers, she never let it go. There are four windows in this room, but you'd never know it because three of them are behind the bookcases."

"So, we're putting the books in the boxes?" Debbie asked. "Any kind of organization?"

"Nope," Dawn said. "But we need to flip through each one. She didn't just use uncashed checks for bookmarks, she used dollar bills too."

They developed a rhythm—remove an armful of books from a shelf, flip through them, pack them away, go back for another armful.

"Do you have enough boxes?" Janet asked as she scooped up a row of paperback westerns.

"More in the next room," Dawn said. "I've been collecting boxes for months."

"Where are the books going?" Debbie asked.

"The library in Yellow Springs will take as many boxes as I cart back home for their yearly used book sale. I suppose I should check with the Dennison library too."

"If the library can't use them," Janet said, "another group in town might want to organize a book sale as a fundraiser."

"Could be," Dawn said. "If you see anything you want, go ahead and take it. Don't spend too much time, though, because I'd like this room finished today." She stopped packing books to wipe her forehead with a sleeve.

"We have our own treasure hunt going on." Janet flipped through her next load of books and told Dawn about getting Eileen's and Ray's input on the quilt blocks and recipe cards. "One of the embroidered names is Thelma Lightwood."

"Is it?" Dawn said. "I had no idea she ever embroidered or quilted."

"Was Thelma related to Nellie?" Debbie asked, using one of the sideways questions she and Janet had decided upon. They knew the answer but hoped the easy question would prompt Dawn to reminisce.

"Thelma was Barbara and Nellie's mother," Dawn said.

"Barbara was your mother-in-law?" Janet asked. "Which sister was older?"

"Nellie." Dawn set another armful of books on the floor beside a box then rubbed the small of her back. "Here's an interesting quirk Nellie developed. One of many. She stopped calling her mother Mom or Mama or Mother and switched to calling her Thelma. Barbara never did that."

"What did Thelma think of that?" Debbie asked.

"She never mentioned it, and I never asked. We weren't terribly close."

That description of a relationship again. Not close. She knew it was easy enough for nieces and nephews to grow apart from aunts and uncles in distant places, but every time she heard Dawn say it, she felt a pang of sorrow. Janet let out a sigh.

"Tired already?" Dawn asked. "We're almost done with this wall."

"Not tired," Janet said. "I was thinking about my own grandmother. She passed more than forty years ago."

"I'm sorry you didn't have her longer," Dawn said.

"Thanks. One of the cards in the box is from her. I made the recipe this morning and it made me feel closer to her."

"That's real nice," Dawn said. If she felt any emotion herself, she didn't show it.

The three worked quietly and steadily. Debbie cleared the last shelf for the day. Janet helped her flip through the books. So far, they'd found nothing more exciting than an old grocery store receipt.

Dawn, staring intently at nothing in particular, dusted her hands on the seat of her pants. "You know," she said, "the first time

I noticed Nellie calling her mother Thelma was after Thelma passed. I wonder what that was all about?"

"Did she ever call her father by his first name?" Debbie asked.

"Not that I recall. If I remember when I get home, I'll ask my daughter. So, who wants to see the footprints?"

They trooped down to the dining room, and Dawn stopped them at the doorway to the kitchen.

"Let's test your powers of deduction," Dawn said. "What do you think the intruder tracked in?"

"Not mud," Debbie said. "I heard that much from Janet. Is that a back porch outside the door? Did something spill out there?"

"You're good at this," Dawn said. "That's an enclosed all-season porch with two or three dozen more trash bags stuffed with *stuff*. Turns out, one of the bags had a small slit near the bottom made by a sharp piece of plastic from a broken toner cartridge from an old printer."

"Loose toner makes an awful mess," Janet said.

"But it doesn't make footprints that last when someone else walks through them like I did," Dawn said. "Come take a look on the porch. The prints next to that bag are crisp and clear."

CHAPTER EIGHT

Janet was glad to see Dawn flip open a deadbolt on the kitchen door that led to the porch. She was also glad to see Debbie quickly snap a picture of the smudges in the kitchen before following her and their hostess out to the porch.

"There." Dawn pointed at two footprints next to the split garbage bag. "What do you think?"

Janet thought Dawn was right. The footprints *were* crisp and clear. "It's interesting that the intruder didn't notice stepping in the toner," she said. "But the footprints stopped right there in the kitchen and didn't go any farther."

"I have a theory about that," Dawn said. "What if the intruder noticed the toner after entering the kitchen and stopped to take off his shoes? He could have crept all over the house, snooping. On the way back out he could have smudged the prints in the kitchen on purpose."

"Then why leave these clear ones out here?" Debbie asked as she took pictures of them.

"Spooked by a noise and ran out?" Dawn said. "Lost his nerve? Just plain didn't notice? People can be pretty oblivious sometimes." Dawn scuffed a foot through the prints and thanked her guests for their help. "You were kind to come." She offered them a smile.

Perhaps Janet and Debbie were making a few holes in Dawn's defensive walls.

Janet and Debbie drove back to the café so Debbie could pick up her car. Before Debbie got out, Janet asked to see the pictures she took of the footprints.

"The prints in the kitchen look more like an inkblot test." Debbie swiped back and forth between the kitchen footprints and the ones on the porch.

"A toner blot test," Janet said.

Debbie swiped back to a picture of a clear footprint on its own. "I'm not an expert in shoe prints, not the way Sherlock Holmes is, but I think the toner prints were also made by an athletic shoe. You know, if Ian weren't so noble, he probably could have told us this and saved us time."

"I know," Janet said. "But where's the fun in that?" Her phone buzzed with a text. "From Mr. Noble himself. Oh bummer. He won't be home for supper and not until late."

"Greg and the boys are busy tonight too. Want to grab dinner together and watch a movie?"

"Sounds like *we* have a date." Janet's phone rang. "Am I popular or what? Oh, it's Eileen. Wait and see what she says. Hi, Eileen."

"Janet, I have good news. I've remembered another of your embroidered names. Even better, the woman lives right here at Good Shepherd."

"Wonderful!"

"If you'd like to meet her, she's available this evening," Eileen said.

Janet heard the hope in Eileen's voice. Eileen got such a kick out of helping them solve mysteries. It was undoubtedly good for her. "Debbie's right here," Janet said. "I'll ask her." Janet put the phone to her chest and relayed the message.

"Let's do it," Debbie said.

Janet grinned. "Eileen? We'd love to meet your friend. How does seven sound?"

"Perfect," Eileen said.

"Good. We'll see you then."

"Shall we take some of the dream bars along?" Debbie asked when Janet disconnected.

Janet smiled. "Sounds like a party."

Upon entering Good Shepherd that evening, Janet saw Eileen sitting in one of the wingback chairs in the reception area. Beside her, in a matching chair, sat a petite, bright-eyed woman wearing a snowman sweatshirt, voluminous sweatpants, and a pair of furry slippers. The chair was big enough to fit two of her. The two white-haired women waved.

"Sign in and come join us," Eileen called.

"We saved you seats," her friend said.

Janet offered the receptionist a dream bar while Debbie signed the visitors' register.

"Thank you!" the receptionist said. "Miss Clary is very excited to meet you. She doesn't get many visitors these days."

"Is it okay for us to have the bars where they're sitting?" Janet asked.

"Perfectly."

"Thanks." Janet signed in, and she and Debbie went to sit with the beaming women.

"Clary Spencer," Eileen said, "I would like you to meet Janet Shaw and Debbie Albright. Janet and Debbie, may I introduce you to my old friend Clary Spencer?"

"We've known each other for years," Clary said.

"We're so happy to meet you," Janet said. "We've brought dessert—dream bars."

"Your grandmother's recipe!" Eileen said. "How did it turn out?"

"A spectacular success," Debbie said. "And although Janet won't brag like that, I didn't have to twist her arm to bring them this evening."

Janet put the cookie bars on paper napkins. Debbie handed one to Clary and another to Eileen. She and Janet watched the other women take their first bites. When the women looked at each other and said, "Oh my," Debbie high-fived Janet and happily dug in.

"Spectacular, indeed," Clary said when Debbie collected and disposed of the napkins. "You bake and, according to Eileen, you two solve mysteries. An exciting combination."

"It's been an interesting time since Debbie moved back to Dennison," Janet said. "Clary, Eileen says that you made one of the quilt blocks we're researching."

"I did. I could hardly believe it when Eileen showed me the pictures of the blocks and there it was. My maiden name, Clarice Graham. That's why Eileen didn't put two and two together when she looked at them. I'd forgotten all about that project, and I don't mind telling you that seeing it again made me quite sentimental."

"I'm sure it did," Debbie said. "What can you tell us about the quilt?"

"I remember the year we made the blocks—1949. Beyond that, I had no real interest in needlework. I never made a quilt myself. And embroidery?" Clary laughed. "Did you notice that my embroidered signature looks more cattywampus than all the others?"

"We didn't notice any such thing." Eileen patted her friend's hand. "If you weren't a quilter, how did you get roped into making a block?"

"I was in the women's circle at my church," Clary said. "We made the quilt as a going-away present."

"Do you remember who the quilt was for?" Janet asked.

"I've had all afternoon to search my old brain for that name, and I finally found it. Donna Collins. Donna and her family were off to California or Florida, one or the other. Someplace sunny, anyway. The quilt was our farewell gift and a way for her family to remember their time in Dennison. A lovely tradition. I wonder if anyone still does that? I wonder if Donna or someone in her family still has the quilt? But then…I don't understand. How is it that you have the blocks?"

"The quilt was never finished," Janet said. "You don't remember that?"

"I don't think I ever knew it." Clary looked stricken, and then her face cleared. "I *can* tell you why I didn't know. For the same reason I'll never forget that we made the blocks in 1949. The day after I finished my block, June 8th, 1949, I had twin boys. I tell you what, I felt like I missed the next several years completely, if not the entire next decade." Clary pretended to fan herself, and the other three laughed.

"Did Eileen show you the pictures of the recipe cards and wedding dress too?" Debbie asked.

"She did, and I'm so sorry but I'm no help with either of them. The dress looks so very 1940s, but I don't recall ever seeing it. As for the recipe cards, the fact that I don't remember might be a clue. The recipes might have been collected during my missing decade." They all laughed again. "So now it's your turn, ladies. Tell me all about how you found the quilt blocks after all these years."

Janet told Clary the story of the trunk and its treasures, their hope to learn more about those treasures, and their desire to know more about the mysterious Nellie.

"Nellie Lightwood." Clary, nodding, sat back, her head nestled in the corner made by the chairback and its wing. "Finding out about her will be easier said than done."

"But you knew her?" Debbie asked.

"Not well. She was older than my boys—I had another boy when the twins were three."

"Oh my," Janet said.

"And another when the twins were four. No more after that—boys, I mean. My daughter came along when the twins were eight. Nellie started teaching in Dennison after my brood graduated high school. We were different generations, but that doesn't always matter."

"Not at all," Eileen agreed, patting Janet's hand.

"Nellie and I served together on an organizational committee for a county chapter of Keep America Beautiful in the late '60s. We ran into each other off and on after that. Both of us were busy the way you are in a small town."

"It takes all hands to care for a small town," Eileen said.

"Isn't that the truth?" Clary said. "From what I could tell, after Nellie retired from teaching, she became somewhat reclusive. I wasn't getting out so much myself, by then, so that might just be my take on it. When I did see her she seemed perfectly happy. So *reclusive* is probably the wrong word."

"Maybe when she retired from teaching, she retired from everything except what pleased her," Eileen said.

Clary nodded. "That could be. What is it they say? She marched to a different drummer. To her own beat."

"That fits with what we've heard from her nephew's wife," Janet said.

"How do you know she was perfectly happy?" Debbie asked.

"Did you know her?" Clary asked.

"We both had her for English in high school," Debbie said. "We never really crossed paths after that."

"But you have fond memories of that class?" Clary tipped her head as she asked.

"It wasn't an easy class," Janet said, "but memorable and very good."

"Think back to that class," Clary said. "How would you describe the usual look on Nellie's face when she was teaching?"

Janet smiled. "Easy. Like she'd just had an amazing idea and couldn't wait to tell us, but she wouldn't, because she wanted us to do our best to discover it for ourselves. She'd lead us right up to the brink."

"And the rest would be up to us," Debbie said.

"That captures the essence of Nellie Lightwood," Clary said. "Self-sufficient and full of life. And it's possible that she didn't understand why other people weren't. Does any of that help you?"

"You might have led us up to the brink," Debbie said with a laugh. "Now we'll have to go home and study."

"Be sure to let me know your conclusion when you reach it."

"Definitely," Janet said. "Do you know if any of the other quilters are still in Dennison?"

"Dorothy Simms," Clary said to a nod from Eileen. "She's still in her own home with daily help. Give her a try, but like many of us, she has good days and bad."

CHAPTER NINE

Supper tonight was Mrs. Bartlett's delicious creamed chipped beef on toast. I know some don't like that dish, but I love it. After supper Dee and Theo picked me up in their father's Ford. It's clean and newer than Grandad's rattletrap truck. Dee calls it the Green Chariot. She drove, I hopped in the front seat beside her, and away we went to a barn dance. Theo had the back seat all to himself. Dee says she never lets Theo drive when they go places together. Not because he's a hazard. She just loves the freedom of driving. Theo asked if I knew how to drive. That's the most direct question he's ever asked me. I told him I can drive a tractor and a truck. He didn't have much to say after that.

Some of the same friends who we picked apples with were at the dance. Lots of other girls and fellas too. It cost us each forty cents to get in. Some of the girls said the barn smelled like horses and made faces. Ridiculous. It might have smelled like clean hay but never horses, because that place was never a real barn. It's just a dance hall built to look like one and decorated with a couple dozen hay bales. Besides, I like how a barn smells—warm and comforting and kind like the cows in our old barn back home before we moved into Steubenville. That town smells like factories. But that smell is good too, Grandad says, because it's the smell of jobs that keep a roof over our heads. And under that roof is the smell of Gran's delicious cooking.

The music set our toes tapping! Three fellas on banjo, fiddle, and bass fiddle had everyone swinging their partners and doing the do-si-do. Then a friend of Dee's put a bug in their ears, and they turned up the swing and the tempo. It turns out that Dee doesn't just love to drive, she loves to dance too. Boy howdy can that gal cut a rug! She should give Theo lessons. He has two left feet. I'm no expert at the jitterbug or the Lindy hop, but even I can keep from tripping my partner or tripping over my partner. He probably can't help it though with those long legs of his.

I'm not an expert on this either, but I think he's sweet on me. Dee says that he is very obviously sweet on me. It is very obvious to me that Dee likes saying very obviously.

Time for an admission. I am sweet on Theo. Every night this week he's walked me home from work holding my hand. He has the kindest brown eyes. When I look into them I can see all the way to his thoughtful nature, his sense of humor, and his deep faith. Mrs. Bartlett took me aside the first night he walked me home and at first I was afraid of what she would say. But she has known Theo since he was a small boy, and she thinks the world of him. That was mighty nice to hear. I've started knitting a scarf for him for Christmas.

October 11, 1941

Dee and I went to see Caught in the Draft *at the movies tonight. Dee said she wanted some laughs, and boy, did it deliver. That's Bob Hope for you. I tried wearing my hair a different way—swirled up with my bangs soft and fluffy. Dee said it was a very sophisticated look. I wore the blue wool pullover that matches my eyes and my tailored gray skirt. A good thing too, because Theo tagged along with us. Dee pretended to be annoyed, but Theo whispered that she'd planned it all along. I told him he could tag along anytime.*

October 12, 1941

After church today, I asked Mrs. Bartlett if I could use her kitchen to bake cookies for Theo. She said she was only too happy and even lent me the recipe for her favorite ones. They're called dream bars. She and I each ate one when I'd finished. They're as dreamy as Theo. I'll give them to him tomorrow.

October 20, 1941

Theo and Dee invited me home for supper. Dee says she's been talking about me to her parents so much that they want to meet me. I'd actually never been to their house, so when we arrived I stopped on the sidewalk and stared. But only for a second because I didn't want to be rude by gawking or showing that I felt very much like a country mouse come to see how the city mice live. Not that Dennison is a city. Steubenville is bigger. But the house is enormous with woodwork curlicues on the porch and above the windows. It's built of red brick and with its white trim it looks like a cake with fancy icing.

Dee and Theo's grandparents built the house, on a big corner lot, in 1906. Theo said the house commands that corner the way an admiral commands his fleet. Then Dee linked arms with me and we marched up the front walk, up the front steps, and sideways through the door.

Inside I wanted to gawk again.

The entryway is all polished wood—parquet floor and wainscotting halfway up the walls. The paint above the wainscotting is dark green. There's a chandelier and a wide stairway to the second floor. The living room is huge with a dark red Turkish carpet and more dark woodwork. The doors between the rooms don't swing; they disappear into the walls. Pocket doors, Theo calls them. Theo says there are six fireplaces in all. Two are downstairs, and there's one in each bedroom upstairs. I wouldn't want to be responsible for cleaning all of them. Dee says there's a maid's room in the attic. Not that they've ever had a maid, but their grandparents had one. The best part of the house is the library. I could spend many happy hours in that snug room—with a fire in the fireplace if the weather was cold.

We ate in the dining room. It's huge too, and the pattern on the wallpaper reminds me of embroidery Gran did on the pillows for our sofa.

Mr. and Mrs. Lightwood have their noses in exactly the same place as Gran and Grandad's country mouse noses—between their eyes and not up in the air. They say the same blessing over the meal as we say at home. Mrs. Lightwood's meal loaf and mashed potatoes were almost, almost as good as Gran's, and her apple dumplings were every bit as good.

Dee and I did the dishes afterward. I wore one of Mrs. Lightwood's aprons and washed while Dee dried. My hostess bustled in and tried to shoo us out, but she didn't succeed. Then Theo came in, and all it took was a whisper in Dee's ear for her to give up and hand him the dish towel. He put on one of his mother's aprons too and rolled up his shirt sleeves.

When we'd finished, Dee, Theo, Mrs. Lightwood, and I played bridge while Mr. Lightwood smoked his *pipe and read his newspaper. Dee said she couldn't bear to hear about the war in Europe after eating apple dumplings. She searched through quite a collection of phonograph records and finally chose Bing Crosby's* Stardust *album. She hummed along to every song, and I think that distracted her just enough so that Theo and I won. Dee and Theo walked me home, and Dee was still humming "Stardust."*

October 25, 1941

I'm a basket of nerves. I've invited Theo home to meet Gran and Grandad.

CHAPTER TEN

*A*t the quiet, tail end of the Saturday lunch hour, Janet and Debbie stood behind the café's counter and worked on the menu for the fashion show. They planned to offer Kim a list of options to choose from for the light luncheon buffet that would be available before the show started.

"How about two kinds of mini quiches—classic quiche Lorraine and broccoli cheddar," Janet said, "Mediterranean pinwheels, stuffed mushroom caps, and avocado goat cheese truffles. Don't the truffles sound amazing? I've been dying to try them."

"That's a lot of round things," Debbie said. "We need options with angles too, so that we're offering a pleasing variety of shapes."

"I think you're reliving the glories of high school geometry again. But you're right." Janet tapped her pencil on her list. "We'll cut the truffles. We can't count on getting perfectly ripe avocados in January anyway. We'll put rectangular ham and cheese tarts in their place. Also cylindrical veggie egg rolls, spinach-feta triangles, and a plate of cheese cubes. Bruschetta topped with fresh mozzarella and fresh tomato relish will add color, and they're ovals, so win-win."

"Do you know what else isn't round?" Paulette asked as she passed with a load of dishes from a bussed table. "Fruit kebabs. Although some of the things on them are round if you include melon balls and grapes. But add pineapple chunks and you've got trapezoids."

"Perfect," Debbie said.

"That's ten options for the light luncheon buffet," Janet said. "We'll ask her to choose seven with an eye for variety of shapes and colors. Now for dessert."

"Let's give her five options and ask her to choose three," Debbie said. "How about mini pecan pies, gingersnaps, dream bars, brownies, and lemon squares?"

"Sounds delicious to me," Janet said. "If she chooses the bars, brownies, and squares, I'll cut the bars in rectangles and the lemon squares in triangles just for you."

"You're a gem," Debbie said. "A gem cut with geometric precision. I'll go type this up and send it to Kim. Have you heard back from Dorothy Simms?"

Janet had called Dorothy the previous afternoon and left a message explaining that Clary Spencer had suggested they call as she might remember working on a quilt, way back in 1949, for Donna Collins. "Not yet," Janet said, looking at her phone in case she'd missed the call.

"I know Dorothy," Paulette said. "I know Willard, her rascally dog, better. She and Willard live the next street over. Her backyard backs up to my neighbor's."

"We heard she has good days and bad," Janet said.

"Her arthritis acts up," Paulette said. "You know, if she didn't recognize your number, she might not listen to your message. Her daughter taught her to be more careful about that. She has my number, though. Would you like me to call her?"

"That would be fabulous, Paulette," Janet said. "If she's up for a visit that would be great. And if she'd be happy to see us this afternoon and you're free, you're welcome to join us."

"Thanks. I always enjoy talking to Dorothy and Willard, but I already have plans. I'm going to try my hand at pickleball."

Janet took over cleaning tables so Paulette could make her call. She admired Paulette's energy and zest for life. It was easy to see that her son Greg came by his own energy and pleasant personality naturally. Debbie was lucky to have found him. *Correction*, Janet thought. *Debbie and Greg are lucky to have found each other.*

Not long after, Paulette called out "Janet?" When Janet looked over, Paulette gave her a thumbs-up. "Three thirty this afternoon. Dorothy asked me to tell you to make sure Willard doesn't escape when you open her front gate, and be sure to close it again behind you. It won't matter how many times you visit her, she'll give the same instructions every time."

"Willard must be an escape artist," Janet said.

Paulette laughed. "Wait till you meet him."

"Shall we take scones?"

"Dorothy's diabetic and is careful with her diet, so better not. Your company will be all she needs to lift her day."

Dorothy Simms must have been watching for Janet and Debbie that afternoon. She opened her front door far enough to stick her head out and call, "Come in, come in, but be careful not to let Willard out when you do. That's him there, beside the rosebush, waiting for his chance to escape. Be sure the gate latches behind you. I can't chase the little dickens all over the neighborhood like I used to." She closed the door.

Janet and Debbie looked at Willard then at each other. Willard, a grizzled old Boston terrier, quite overweight, looked no more likely to escape than Dorothy was to chase him. They followed instructions, however, latching the gate securely behind them. They said hello to Willard, who yawned and followed them slowly up the front walk to the house. Dorothy, smiling, repeated her, "Come in, come in," and Janet, Debbie, and a dawdling Willard stepped inside.

"So you two own the Whistle Stop Café," Dorothy said when they were all sitting in her comfortable living room. "I've haven't made it there yet, but Paulette says she'll take me one day."

"We would love to see you there," Debbie said.

"Paulette also says that you have questions about an unfinished quilt."

"We do," Janet said. "We have a set of blocks that were meant to be an autograph quilt with embroidered names. You made one of them." She opened her tablet and brought up the picture of Dorothy's square. "Do you remember this?" She showed her the picture.

"I certainly do. A labor of love." Dorothy put her hands to her heart. "I would dearly love to see those blocks again."

"You can see them when Paulette brings you to the café," Debbie said. "They're at the depot museum. Do you know why the quilt was never finished? Clary Spencer knew you were making it for Donna Collins, who planned to move away. Clary didn't know that the quilt wasn't finished and thought you might know why."

Dorothy nodded. "A sad story. For Donna's sake, those of us who knew it hushed it up. But that was so long ago that I don't see how it can hurt anyone to tell it now." Dorothy settled more comfortably into her chair, Willard at her feet. "Donna Collins was a military wife. During the war, her husband, Wayne, served overseas. She and her young children came to stay with her sister in Dennison. Donna was a sweet young woman and the children, a boy and two girls, were cute as buttons. She volunteered at the canteen several times a week, handing out sandwiches and doughnuts and all. You might find her in some of the pictures at the museum. When the war ended, Wayne received an honorable discharge, and they decided to stay in Dennison."

Willard yawned, rose, and went to lie down with his head on Janet's foot, where he started to drool.

"Willard, you scamp!" Dorothy said. "Come here."

Willard heaved himself up and returned to her feet.

"Now, where was I?" Dorothy asked.

"Donna and Wayne decided to stay in Dennison," Janet said.

"That's right. We were all glad of that. Donna was a wonderful and faithful member of the church. She loved being part of our women's sewing circle. The children were polite and well brought up. That started to change after Wayne came home from the war. Donna and the children became quiet. The boy started getting into fights at school. Wayne worked first at a filling station. After a few months he left that job and went to work for the railroad. He quit after a year or so and started working in construction. In the spring of 1949, Donna told us that Wayne had announced they would move at the end of the summer, after he finished the construction project he was on. He'd get paid big, and then they'd get out. Get away. Make a fresh start."

"Clary said she heard they were going someplace sunny," Debbie said. "California or Florida."

"Texas," Dorothy said. "Things looked happier for them as they made plans. Donna and the children smiled more. The sewing circle decided to make a going-away present for her—a signature quilt. We hoped it would be a nice way for her to remember us and her time in Dennison. Practical too. Even sunny places get cold sometimes." Willard lay like a lead weight on her feet, snoring softly.

"We got as far as collecting the squares," she continued, "which hadn't taken long to make with each of us doing one. But before we got them stitched together, much less finished the quilt, the family up and disappeared one night without a word. End of June, that was. Not even the *middle* of summer. It was incredibly sad, and no one ever heard from her again, so far as I know. As I said, those of us who suspected or knew what was going on in that sad family kept it hushed up. You can't always hush things up in a small town, but Dennison was bigger back then."

"Did you know what was going on?" Debbie asked quietly.

Dorothy's lips thinned. "We call it domestic abuse now. Wayne would apologize and promise it would stop. Donna would forgive. A vicious, terrible circle. And so many of our young men came back from the war changed. How could they not be?" Dorothy reached down to rub Willard between his ears. With a sigh she sat back up. "But that story is water long, long gone under the bridge. What other questions have you got for me?"

"We have another picture for you to look at," Janet said. She scrolled to the wedding dress and showed Dorothy. "Do you recognize this dress? Remember anyone wearing it or talking about a dress like this? We think it was never worn, if that jogs something in your memory."

Dorothy stared at the dress long and hard but shook her head. "I'm sorry. Is this also at the museum?"

"It is," Debbie said. "We found it and the quilt blocks in a trunk that came from Nellie Lightwood's attic. Did you know her?"

"We were just acquaintances, not what I'd call friends, but yes, I knew her."

"How would you describe her?" Janet asked.

"Secretive—but secretive in a good way that brought joy to others." Dorothy's eyes strayed to a colorfully painted vase on an end table. "I found that vase in front of my door early one morning with a beautiful bouquet of wildflowers in it. This was a month after my husband died, and the flowers were such a lovely memory of him. He loved his garden. He even won a garden-of-the-month award. The flowers at my door were a joyful pick-me-up."

"They must have been," Debbie said.

"I was never certain, but I thought Nellie might have left the vase and flowers."

"What made you think that?" Janet asked.

"I'm pretty sure I remember being attracted to this vase at a yard sale earlier in that year that my husband passed. The vase was broken, though. Had a chip on the rim and a good long crack. Nellie was there too, and I think she bought it along with a few other... shall we say, less-than-perfect things? But if you look at the vase now, the rim and the crack are mended. Not invisibly, but with repairs that draw attention so you know the vase is loved and probably more beautiful than before because of the flaws. I might not be saying that very well."

"You said it very well," Janet said. "My grandmother used to say that wrinkles are beauty marks that show how much we care about each other." She ran a finger down the mended crack in the vase. "A crack made beautiful by mending is the same thing."

"That's it," Dorothy said. "Nellie and her red wagon were a fixture at yard sales and rummage sales, often taking home the rejects, happy to exchange smiles if not always the time of day. The flowers at my door were a definite smile."

"Do you know who ended up with the quilt blocks?" Debbie asked. "We found them in a trunk, and we're trying to figure out who owned the trunk. Could Thelma Lightwood have kept them?"

"She certainly could have, but I'd be surprised if she did," Dorothy said. "Thelma's first love, after her family, was her garden. I think someone more interested in quilting would have kept the blocks."

"Ada Carpenter made one of the squares," Janet said. "Do you know if she's still in Dennison? Or any of the others who made squares?"

"Ada's son in Columbus moved her to a memory care facility there, last spring. Ada incorporated wonderful, rich colors and traditions from the African-American experience into her quilts. Things her mother and grandmother taught her, like depicting biblical stories in the quilt squares. It was amazing. So many of the others are gone now. But did you know that there's a group of quilters who meet every week in the programming room at the library?"

"No." Janet and Debbie shook their heads.

"Most of them are youngsters with better eyesight than mine and wild ideas about patterns," Dorothy said. "It may still be worth asking if any of them are in touch with the older generation of quilters. They might have known some of the women who worked on Donna's quilt."

"That's a great lead," Janet said. "Thank you. If they don't know anything, they might be able to give us other leads."

"There you go," Dorothy said. "One stitch at a time is how we accomplish anything."

"Do you think quilts like this were ever mentioned in the newspaper?" Janet asked.

"I suppose they might have been written up in the social column," Dorothy said, "but only after they were given away. If a quilt was meant to be a gift, a surprise, you wouldn't want it in the paper ahead of time, would you?"

"That makes perfect sense," Janet said, laughing at herself.

"We're not any closer to knowing about the wedding dress," Debbie said as Janet drove her back to the depot to pick up her car. "It feels like one dead end after another."

"We haven't been at it for very long," Janet said. "So not *that* many dead ends. We did learn a lot more about the quilt. Just not how Nellie got hold of the squares."

"Here's a reason Thelma might still have had the blocks," Debbie said. "Someone more interested in quilting might have finished the quilt. Not for Donna but for someone else."

"Good point. We have another lead too. After I drop you off, I'm going to the library to find out when the quilters meet there. Unless you want to come along?"

"I'd better get home and do something exciting like the laundry."

"Don't get too wild with that." Janet pulled into the depot parking lot. Before Debbie opened the car door, Janet put a hand on her arm. "When we have setbacks, or don't learn as much as we want to, let's not think of it as a dead end. Let's think of the investigation as a maze, and when we get stopped, we'll think of it as an opportunity to turn around and find another path."

"You, my friend," Debbie said, "are a-maz-ing. Let me know what you learn at the library."

Ellie Cartwright, the head librarian, greeted Janet when she entered the building. Janet knew firsthand what a whiz Ellie was at finding whatever information she needed on any pertinent database. Knowing Ohio history was her superpower. Ellie had also been two years behind Janet in school so, after learning that the quilting group met on Mondays, Janet asked her if she'd had Nellie Lightwood for a teacher.

"She was a blast, wasn't she?" Ellie said. "I loved it when I found out her first name was Nellie. Ellie and Nellie. Goodness, I loved that English class." Ellie absently stuck another pen into her messy bun, making it a collection of three.

Janet pictured the bun starting out neat and contained in the morning and gradually relaxing throughout the day to finally achieve the marvelous look of librarian chic that Ellie carried off so well. "Did you keep in contact with her after high school?" Janet asked.

"No, and she didn't come into the library very often. I always pictured her spending her evenings, weekends, and vacations in her own fabulous library surrounded by books."

"You probably weren't far off. Debbie and I helped Nellie's niece box up some of the books at the house. Her niece might contact you to see if you want books for a sale."

"That'd be great."

"I haven't come across anyone yet who says they really knew Nellie," Janet said. "You wouldn't think someone could be so invisible in a town this size."

"I doubt she was," Ellie said. "I bet she was like the books that people can't find on our shelves. All it takes is the right eyes to find them. Say, have you heard about the special exhibition basketball game at the high school tonight?"

Janet shook her head.

"You should go. A team of former star Mustangs, calling themselves the Old Gray Nags, are taking on the varsity boys for charity."

"That might be an uneven game if the former stars are full-grown men in their twenties," Janet said.

"Something tells me the boys will keep the Old Gray Nags on their toes, no matter how old they turn out to be," Ellie said with a laugh. "A lot of alumni are putting on their Mustang orange and black and going. It might be a good opportunity to ask around about Nellie."

CHAPTER ELEVEN

Ian and Janet pulled into the Claymont High School parking lot that evening. Janet was by the number of cars already there.

"Quite a turnout," Ian said. "I hope we can still get tickets."

"I didn't even think about that," Janet said just as her phone buzzed with a text. "But leave it to Debbie! She worried about tickets too, so she bought ours. We can pick them up at the table. She and Greg are sitting in the middle on the visitors' side of the gym."

"Very thoughtful," Ian said, and they followed a trail of orange and black hoofprints to the Claymont Mustangs' gym.

They retrieved their tickets and waited in line at the door to get their hands stamped. Then Ian slipped his arm through Janet's, saying, "I'd hate to lose you in this crowd."

Janet laughed. "Stick with me, Chief, and I'll make sure you don't get swept away in a Mustang stampede. I wonder how hard it'll be to find Debbie?"

"Not hard at all," Ian said. "Look." He pointed then waved back to Greg's younger son, eighth-grader Julian, waving wildly to catch their attention.

"I saved your seats for you," Julian called as Janet and Ian stepped between people to climb the bleachers.

"Thank you," Janet said. "It's good to see you. This is exciting, isn't it?"

"Yep." Julian hopped up and, with a quick look at his dad, said, "I mean, yes ma'am. Bye!" He raced down the bleachers and across the basketball court to sit with his brother. Jaxon, a sophomore at Claymont and not quite so exuberant as Julian, still managed to return Janet's and Ian's waves.

"I love the way your boys get along, Greg." Janet slid in next to Debbie, and Ian plunked down next to her.

"They have their moments, believe me," Greg said. "But tonight I told them the longer they get along the more I'll donate to the class bucket. There's a pizza party riding on this for the class collecting the most in donations tonight. Julian's gung-ho for the sophomores to win even though he won't get the pizza."

Ian laughed. "Maybe he knows you'll spring for a private pizza party at home. What charity is the money going to?"

"Cincinnati Children's Hospital," Debbie said. "With this crowd it should be a sizable donation. When Julian and Jaxon saw the number of people arriving, they were afraid you might not get in."

"They're a couple of sweethearts," Janet said.

"With ulterior motives," said Greg. "If you tell the volunteers at the concession stand which class you're supporting, they'll add your purchase to that class's total."

"Count us in," Ian said. "And thanks for getting the tickets. What do we owe you?"

"Don't worry about that," Debbie said. "You can buy the first round of snacks."

"Deal," Ian said. "I'll avoid the crowd and hit the stand when the game starts."

"Debbie and I have an ulterior motive for being here too," Janet said. She told Ian and Greg their plan to ask other alumni for their memories of Nellie Lightwood.

"We keep hoping we'll hear something about the trunk and its contents, specifically the wedding dress," Debbie said. "Barring that, maybe we'll get a lead on someone else to ask or somewhere else to look."

"You think you might get information about a seventy- or eighty-year-old wedding dress at a basketball game?" Greg asked, a bit skeptically.

"I have it on good authority that the best detectives leave no avenue unexplored, no stone unturned," Debbie said. "Isn't that right, Chief Shaw?"

"Correct," Ian said. "I would only add no basketball undribbled."

"So-o-o-o," Janet said, stretching out the word and glancing between the two men. "We'd love it if you two would ask around during halftime too. Not about the wedding dress, if you don't want to, although that would be great too. Mainly for memories of Ms. Lightwood. A lot of the older fans in the audience must have had her for English. You might find someone who kept up with her more recently."

"If you're worried that people will wonder why you're asking," Debbie said, "tell them it's connected to the fashion show at the Dennison Depot Museum at the end of the month. The show wouldn't have come about without Nellie."

"You don't have to worry about explaining the fashion show either," Janet said. "Debbie and I just happen to have these." She pulled a sheaf of flyers from her purse. "Hand them out to anyone who expresses interest. It'll be good advertising."

"We'll give it the old Claymont High School try," Greg said with a twinkle in his eyes. "And then Ian and I can add fashion promoter to our résumés."

"All in the line of duty," Ian said.

The PA system crackled to life, and a disembodied voice gained the attention of the audience. "Welcome, everyone, to the first ever exhibition game featuring our current boys' varsity team and a team of former Mustangs, all the way from the wilds of Cincinnati, calling themselves the Old Gray Nags. Please join me in putting your hands together for the Claymont Mustang boys' varsity team!"

The boys, stringy and serious, ran single file from the locker room. They ran two laps around the outside of the court to cheers from the Claymont cheer squad and huge applause from the fans in the bleachers on both sides. They took seats on their bench and turned expectantly toward the visitors' locker room.

"Now let's all wish the men of the Old Gray Nags best of luck!" said the announcer.

As the team came out onto the floor, Ian and Greg exchanged looks. Two of the men ran out and around the court. The rest ambled. These were definitely not the twentysomethings Janet had predicted earlier.

Some wore Bermuda shorts and Hawaiian shirts, a few had dressed in their old Mustang uniforms, one wore a three-piece suit and carried a heart-shaped box and a bouquet of roses, and the rest wore cutoff sweatpants or baggy shorts and Old Gray Nag T-shirts with a whiskery, gray version of the Claymont Mustang on the front. One player limped, another sported thick-lensed glasses and wandered in a circle at the center of the court, and a third had his arm in a sling. They were enthusiastically cheered on by a group of former cheerleaders, one of whom looked to be at least eighty and was smiling broadly. The player with the glasses was introduced as the game's guest referee.

"I think we're in for quite a show." Ian settled back. "I'm glad we came."

The referee blew his whistle for the tip-off. A tall, sinewy boy from the Mustangs bounced to the inner circle, looking like he had springs in his legs. The Nag wearing the suit ran to join him, holding the roses and heart-shaped box over his head like trophies. He handed them to the referee, who sniffed the bouquet and stuck it in his back pocket. He stuffed the box into his tucked-in shirt and tossed the basketball up between the players. The Nags won the tip-off. Athletic chaos ensued.

The visiting team's unorthodox uniforms didn't hold them back. Neither did the limp. The Nag with the sling played one-armed throughout—and played well. The antics of the Nags rivaled the best from the highly skilled, comedic Harlem Globetrotters. The Mustang players were being soundly trounced.

"Part of the Mustangs' problem," Debbie said, wiping away tears of laughter, "is that they're laughing as hard as the rest of us."

At halftime the captain of the Old Gray Nags brought a microphone to the center of the court. As would befit the captain of a team, he was the man in the suit. He'd reclaimed his roses and heart box from the referee. "We're all former Mustangs and remember our high school basketball time fondly. As chance would have it, after high school or university, each of us ended up living and working in

Cincinnati. Over the years we found each other and came up with the idea of putting together a team of old Mustangs. We started playing together for fun. Then we discovered our talent for making audiences laugh and got the idea to bring our show home to Dennison." He paused for a round of applause.

"It isn't all fun and games, though. The proceeds from this match between the excellent current Mustangs and their doddering elders, who are all on the way to the glue factory, are going to the Cincinnati Children's Hospital. That includes sales at the concession stand. Halftime will last for an extended period to let you generously empty your pockets for a snack and to give the Nags a much-needed nap." Chuckles and outright laughter sounded from the stands, including from Janet and her group.

"Before I let you go, I have two interesting pieces of trivia. First is that the youngest Nag is fifty, and that isn't me. Second is that my wife and I are celebrating our forty-fifth wedding anniversary today." He held out his arm and one of the Nag cheerleaders joined him in the center. He knelt and handed her the roses and the box. The audience gave them a standing ovation.

When that quieted down, Ian said, "Good thing they extended halftime. I was having too much fun and forgot to beat the crowd."

"More time for us to talk to people too," Debbie said.

"If people can't remember much on the spur of the moment," Janet said, "let's tell them to contact us at the café if they do come up with something."

"Good idea," Debbie said. "Split up or go together?"

"We'll cover more ground if we split up," Greg said, taking a handful of fashion show flyers from her. "Meet you back here."

Janet watched Greg bound down the bleachers looking like a grown-up version of Julian. "It's no wonder his sons are such good kids," she said.

Debbie looked thoughtful, and Janet wondered what she was thinking. After a moment, she said, "Let's go. And let's hope we find some answers."

Janet followed her friend to the floor, where they went in opposite directions. She found it easy to approach people and break the ice with the flyers. They'd decided to target people their age and older, even though they might miss of a few of Nellie's old students that way.

Ellie waved when she saw Janet ten minutes later. "Isn't this a hoot?" she said. "How's the memory collecting going?"

"I'd forgotten all about when the theater kids put on *The Miracle Worker*," Janet said. "The last person I talked to reminded me. I wasn't in the production, but Nellie had her English classes read the play. I've never forgotten her favorite Helen Keller quote: 'Keep your face to the sunshine and you cannot see a shadow.' I love that."

"It's so Nellie. I'll talk to people too, if you'd like."

"Thanks!" Janet told her about the flyers and gave her a handful.

Janet continued to circulate, running into classmates she hadn't talked to in ages and meeting Nellie's students from classes before her own time. It seemed they'd all gone on with their own lives after graduating and hadn't kept in touch with Nellie. Hearing that was bittersweet for Janet. At least she wasn't alone in losing touch, but the more glimpses she got of Nellie's life, the more insights she wished she had.

"She was a character, wasn't she?" a woman ten years ahead of Janet said. "She was also very kind. When I was going through a tough time junior year, she took me aside and told me something she learned from her dad—to always leave a margin for the unexpected and to be open to surprises and joy."

Janet had remembered that advice too. Now it made her think of the anonymous mittens and hats being left around town. Certainly they were unexpected, and they were likely to bring joy to whomever found them. If Nellie were still alive, Janet would guess she was behind the random gifts, but of course it had to be someone else. She started asking people if they'd noticed them, and from a few people she heard memories, like Patricia's, of the earlier anonymous artist.

"I've heard it wasn't just knitted things," Janet said to a woman who remembered her parents telling stories about anonymous art.

"My aunt received embroidered napkins," she said. "There were other kinds of arts-and-crafts projects too. Repainted chairs and stools. Mom heard about an old milk crate decorated so beautifully it was a piece of folk art."

A man who'd looked after his father when he'd broken his hip remembered finding a walker and a cane on the front porch. "Painted like a barber pole," he said. "Both of them, and that was perfect for Dad because he'd been a barber his whole working life. I never did find out who brought them."

"About once a week I'd see something on the bench at the depot," a woman said. "Mended, painted flowerpots, a teapot and single cup and saucer once, mostly mittens and hats. And then it stopped."

"When?" Janet asked.

"A couple of years ago? I don't remember. But it's picked back up again. The mittens and hats, anyway. I haven't heard of anything else. Have you?"

"I haven't," Janet said. "But I'd like to."

"So would I!"

"Do you think it's the original anonymous artist?" Janet asked.

"That's a good question." The woman stared toward the basketball hoop as she thought, and then shook her head. "Any time I saw something on the bench I looked at it. Never took anything home with me and regretted it a few times. Those flowerpots I said were mended? Even the mending was beautiful. But there's something different about the mittens and hats, now. Almost like every knitter has a signature. Does that make sense? When I started seeing them again, it's like the signature had changed. Not wildly, but enough to make me wonder if someone new picked up where the original knitter left off."

"Do you know who the original was?" Janet asked.

"It's more fun not knowing, don't you think?" The woman put her hand on Janet's arm. "Thank you. This has been so much fun dredging up memories. I'll definitely come to the fashion show."

"It was my pleasure. Thank *you*."

An announcement came over the public address system letting the audience know the extended halftime would end in five minutes. Janet saw Debbie, Greg, and Ian heading back to the bleachers, Ian with his arms full of bags of popcorn. Rejoining them, Janet learned they'd each heard similar memories of Nellie and had handed out all their flyers. No one they'd spoken to had any clues about the wedding dress. Ellie joined them, and when she told them what she'd heard, they agreed she'd picked up the best tidbit of the evening—in her retirement, Nellie had continued volunteering for the high school's theater department and did so up until shortly before her death.

"The theater teacher's name is Courtney McCampbell," Ellie said. "Does that help?"

"That's definitely worth following up," Janet said. "Thanks."

Ellie returned to her own seat just as Julian and Jaxon came to check in with Greg. The boys each happily accepted a bag of popcorn, plus one extra.

"Hey, Jaxon," Debbie said, "you're not involved in theater at school, right?"

"Right, but Piper is."

"Who's Piper?" Debbie asked.

"A girl in my class. She's sitting with us."

"Do you think she'd mind if Janet and I talk to her? We wouldn't want to come across as weird, nosy adults."

Jaxon guffawed. "You aren't weird, and Piper is right over..." He turned to look for her then shrugged. "She's here somewhere. If I find her I'll let you know. Okay if we sit on the other side again, Dad?"

"Sure thing. See you after."

The second half of the game was just as entertaining as the first. The Old Gray Nags won by a single basket. All the players took bows to a standing ovation. Two of the Nags lay down on the floor pretending they'd passed out.

Julian and Jaxon met up with Greg, Debbie, Janet, and Ian on the floor after they left the bleachers. Julian held two empty popcorn bags and was finishing the third.

"Did you eat all three bags?" Greg asked.

Julian held up two fingers. "Jaxon was going to give this one to Piper, but she disappeared after halftime—poof—just like the Old Gray Nag's massive lead."

"They still won," Jaxon said.

Julian grinned. "That winning basket was amazing. From the middle of the court, and it went straight in!" He jumped high and threw an imaginary basketball. "They were so cool. Old like Dad and Chief Shaw, but way cool."

Greg and Ian looked at each other and shrugged.

"Oh hey, there's Piper heading for the door," Jaxon said. "In the orange hoodie. Piper!"

It wasn't quite a *sea* of orange hoodies in front of them, but there were a lot, and none of the girls wearing one turned around when Jaxon called Piper's name. Janet saw one girl push her way past a gaggle of others, though, and quickly disappear.

CHAPTER TWELVE

*K*im bopped into the café Monday morning and made herself comfortable on a stool at the counter. "Coffee, please," she said to Debbie, "and one of whatever heavenly thing Janet baked. I could eat that smell just on its own."

"You're cheery this morning," Janet said, putting an apple cinnamon streusel-top muffin on a plate for her.

"Funny how that works on a day off," Kim said. She took a bite of the warm muffin and closed her eyes. "I was right. Heaven."

"We know something new about Nellie," Debbie said.

"About the trunk or anything in it?" Kim asked.

"No, but we have a lead."

"Detective lingo," Kim said. "Always a good sign coming from you two. What's the lead?"

"Nellie was still volunteering for the high school theater teacher up until shortly before she passed," Debbie said. "What's the teacher's name, Janet?"

"Courtney McCampbell. I'll give her a call and see when she's free. Maybe she got to know Nellie, and maybe they talked about more than props and productions."

"Worth a shot," Kim said. She finished her muffin and thanked Debbie when she topped off her coffee. "I've made my choices for the fashion show menu, although you didn't help by making everything sound scrumptious."

"We can't help it," Janet said. "It's a gift. What did you choose?"

"Let's cut the stuffed mushroom caps, the Mediterranean pinwheels, or one of the mini quiches," Kim said. "You can choose which one. For dessert let's go with dream bars, lemon squares, and brownies."

"Perfect," Janet said making quick notes. "Have you lined up your models?"

"It won't hurt to find two or three more, but I'm getting there," Kim said. "Are you sure you can't ask someone else to help Paulette serve the food so I can put you in the show too?"

"Only if you really can't find someone else, and I'm sure you can. I'll feel better making sure the buffet runs smoothly. Besides, Debbie will represent the café in the show by wearing the wedding dress."

"Have I agreed to that?" Debbie asked.

"Yes," Kim and Janet said in tandem.

"Hmm. Sometimes I think my memory isn't as good as Eileen's," said Debbie.

"But you will wear it, won't you?" asked Kim.

Debbie hesitated for a moment then said, "Yes."

Soon after, Debbie disappeared into the kitchen. Kim said quietly to Janet, "I bet Greg would like to hear Debbie say yes someday too."

That afternoon, Janet called the high school and was put through to Courtney McCampbell. Courtney had a bright, energetic voice and said she'd be happy to talk to Janet about Nellie.

"Can you come to the high school tomorrow afternoon?" Courtney asked. "We just cast the spring musical. We're doing *Guys and Dolls*. You might enjoy hearing the students practicing their lines."

"Will you be in the auditorium?" Janet asked.

"We will. From three o'clock until who knows when," Courtney said with a laugh.

"Thanks. See you tomorrow then." Janet disconnected and headed for the library to find out if the quilting group had a few minutes to spare for show and tell. She had brought her tablet so she could show them the pictures of the quilt blocks if they were interested.

Ellie smiled when Janet walked through the library door. "Here to see the quilters?" she asked. "They're just settling into the program room. I let them know they might have a visitor. You know where the room is?"

"Sure do. Thanks, Ellie." Janet made her way to the program room. The door was open, and she chuckled over Dorothy's description of the quilters as youngsters. Janet guessed that only two or three of the dozen women were younger than sixty.

Three long tables had been pushed together to make a square in the middle of the room, and the women sat around it. Some of them worked at whirring sewing machines, while others measured and cut fabric on gridded cutting boards. Two women had set up portable quilting frames and stitched by hand. Soft conversation filled the room. Janet felt, for a moment, like she had stepped into a women's sewing circle fifty, a hundred, or a hundred and fifty years ago. The modern tools, bright and bold fabrics, and the women's hairstyles and clothing brought her back to the present.

Janet knocked on the door frame. Heads turned. Smiles and voices around the table invited her in.

"Only if I won't disrupt your work," Janet said.

"Not at all," a woman wearing a quilted vest said. "Hi, I'm Lois. Part of the reason we meet at the library is so people will stop and learn a little about what we love doing."

"That and so we can be nosy and see what everyone else is working on," another woman said. "And gossip."

"We don't gossip," the woman across from her said. "We exchange community news."

The quilters laughed and asked Janet what she was most interested in—quilting, being nosy, or community news.

"A bit of all three," Janet said. She told them what she, Debbie, and Kim knew about the unfinished autograph quilt then watched and listened to their reactions as they passed her tablet around the table, scrolling through the pictures of the blocks.

"You couldn't bring the blocks with you?" Lois asked. "My fingers ache to touch them."

"I wish I could have," Janet said. "While the museum decides what to do with them, they're staying safely there."

Several of the older women recognized some of the embroidered names. Janet made note of those names, and then she saw that the woman who now held the tablet was wiping her eyes. Lois noticed too.

"Rita, oh my goodness." Lois moved her chair next to Rita's and handed her a handkerchief. "What is it, dear?"

Rita looked up at the concerned faces. "This is my block."

Lois took the tablet from her. "Margherita D'Amato."

"My maiden name," Rita said. "I recognize so many of these other names too, most of them gone. And it was so incredibly sad to lose a friend like that. Donna was here, then overnight she was gone and we never heard from her again." She dabbed at her eyes. "I hated that we didn't have a chance to finish the quilt for her."

"I'm so sorry I've caused you distress, Rita," Janet said.

"Oh, sweetheart, my tears aren't from distress. They're what's leaking out from the flood of memories."

"Do you know who kept the squares when the quilt was set aside?" Janet asked.

"People got quite cranky over the whole thing," Rita said. "I never did like confrontations, so I stayed out of it."

"Rita's only recently moved back to Dennison," Lois said.

"After my husband died," Rita said. "To make it easier for my son."

"And it isn't easy making a move at our age, is it?" Lois said.

"That's why I'm grateful for all of you," Rita said to the quilters. "I haven't done any quilting in years, and my fingers don't work quite as well as they used to, but I've been so lonely since moving back and you accepted me like we're old friends."

"Like we're comfortable, old quilts," Lois said. "Even you young ones among us with your wild and crazy colors and patterns."

"I love all of that," Rita said. "The colors and patterns you use reflect your bright and loving natures."

The quilters applauded Rita's speech.

"May I show you something else?" Janet asked.

"Please do!" Rita said, the others nodding.

"Among the other things we found in the trunk, with the quilt squares, is an old recipe box." Janet took the tablet and brought up pictures of the box. She handed the tablet back to Rita.

With several others looking over her shoulders, Rita scrolled through the recipes then stopped. "Look at that," she said. "My recipe for pineapple upside-down cake. That's the recipe that won my Virgil's heart." Rita passed the tablet to the next quilter and said, "I don't think the recipe box is like quilt squares."

"How do you mean?" Janet asked.

"From the pictures, some of the recipes look like they were jotted down, not written out with the care you'd take if it was for a special occasion, a gift. I think your box of recipes is a private collection."

"That's what we think too," Janet said. "Rita, did you know Thelma Lightwood?"

"Thelma! I haven't thought about Thelma Lightwood in years. In decades. Now there was a spry gal, and oh how she loved to cook."

"Could the box have belonged to her?"

"Well now, it might at that," Rita said. "Quite a few of those recipes, like mine, have someone's name on them. But not all. If you can find something Thelma wrote, you can compare her handwriting to the anonymous recipes."

"Didn't I see that name on one of the quilt squares?" asked Lois.

"Did you?" Rita said. "I guess after I found my own I was so overcome I never looked at the rest. So now you have a sample of her handwriting, Janet, and what you need is a handwriting expert."

A light bulb went off in Janet's head. A handwriting expert—that's what she'd been thinking about then swiftly forgotten when Kim went off on her cursive writing tangent at Eileen's Wednesday evening.

The light bulb became the headlight of Janet's train of thought hurtling down its tracks. At this point they didn't need a true professional, but what if they could identify the person who wrote the note tucked into the wedding dress by comparing that handwriting to the quilt signatures, the handwritten recipes, and the two-part notes? Would that tell them who the dress had belonged to?

The wedding dress! Janet took the tablet again, scrolled to the pictures of the garment, and asked if, by any remote chance, any of them recognized it. The tablet went around the table again, with many admiring remarks about the cut and style, but they were all sorry to say they didn't remember ever seeing it.

"I've got good news for you," Janet said. "If you'd like to see the wedding dress in person, and the other clothes we found in the trunk, the Dennison Depot Museum and the Whistle Stop Café are having a fashion show. I brought flyers about it in case you'd like to come. And now, I need to let you get back to your work. Thank you for letting me take up so much of your time this afternoon. I can't tell you how much I appreciate it."

Lois left the room with Janet and took her aside out of earshot of the quilters. "Thank you for coming to see us today, Janet. Rita said more today than she's said since she joined the group. She's sweet as she can be but has been somewhat lost since losing her husband and then coming back here."

"She said she came back to make it easier for her son. Is she living with him?" Janet asked.

Lois shook her head. "That's what I don't understand. She moved into Good Shepherd. It's a wonderful place. She should be meeting all kinds of people. I worry that she's been staying in her room."

"That thought breaks my heart," Janet said. "I know some lovely people at Good Shepherd. I'll tell them to find her. What's her last name?"

"Chaffee," Lois said. "Thank you, Janet."

Janet left the library thinking their luck might be changing in their search for the stories behind their trunk treasures. Before she drove home, she called Eileen at Good Shepherd and asked her to introduce herself, Ray, and Clary to Rita Chaffee.

Tuesday morning, Janet hustled from her car through the biting, pre-dawn cold to the café—but abruptly stopped when she saw a gift bag sitting on one of the benches on the station platform. The wrapping didn't look at all threatening, but the sight was unexpected. She went closer for a better look and couldn't help breaking into a grin. Her luck from yesterday must be holding. A tag pinned to the bag read, *Please take me home or give me to someone who needs me.* She opened the bag and found a beautiful knit hat in a whirl of wild colors.

Janet didn't need a new hat, but she knew someone who might enjoy the charming, vivid creation. She placed the hat on her head and unlocked the door to the café to start her baking for the day.

Later, Debbie arrived with compliments for the aroma Janet's scones, muffins, and cookies had conjured, and headed for the office. Janet didn't have long to wait before she heard Debbie say, "What's this?" and then exclaim, "Oh my goodness, you found one!" She came out of the office with the hat in her hands. "It's gorgeous. In an abstract kind of way. Where did you find it?"

"Sitting on one of the benches on the platform. I waited for you before studying at it more closely. Remember what one of the women at the basketball game told me about the 'signature' of the anonymous artist changing? Does this hat tell you anything about the person who knitted it?"

Debbie studied the hat. "I'm no knitting expert, but I don't think there's anything fancy about these stitches. It's the textures of the yarn and the colors that make it wild, woolly, and fun." She placed it on a counter Janet wasn't using.

Janet took a pan of scones from the oven then came to look at the hat. "I don't see any rhyme or reason to how the colors are used, do you? Wait—look right there in the middle." She wiped her finger on her apron then traced the subtle pattern she'd found. "It's an *N*, isn't it? *N* for Nellie?"

"Whoa," Debbie said. "You could be right."

Janet felt a tingle of excitement. "It's a long shot, but I'm going to take the hat to Sticks & Threads this afternoon. Maybe Bonnie sells yarn like this."

"It can't hurt to ask," Debbie said. "While you're there, see if she's had any luck tracking down fabric like the flour sacking in the old apron."

"Want to come with me? We can go from there to the high school and talk to Courtney McCampbell."

"Yes!" Debbie said. "I think we're getting somewhere, don't you?"

Janet parked in front of the craft shop in Uhrichsville, not much more than a hop, skip, and a jump from the Whistle Stop Café. Sticks & Threads, located in one of the beautiful old redbrick buildings in Uhrichsville, sold fabric, yarn, notions and more. Janet saw fabrics in the window display like some she'd seen the quilters at the library using. A bell tinkled over the door when Debbie opened it.

Bonnie looked up from cutting fabric for a customer and smiled. "Nice to see you two. I'll be right with you."

Debbie nudged Janet and pointed her chin toward one of the yarn displays. They went over for a closer look.

"So many beautiful colors," Debbie said.

"Some of them look good enough to eat," Janet agreed. She took the hat from the bakery bag she'd placed it into and compared it to a display of handspun yarns. They were gorgeous. Many of them consisted of two or three colors twisted together. Some were as woolly as caterpillars.

"They're just as soft as they look," Debbie said, stroking a skein of pink and orange yarn.

Excited, Janet put the hat back in the bag. "I think we've found the source for the hat's yarn," she said. "It has the same feel if not the exact same shades. Look, Bonnie's free now. Come on."

Janet reached the sales counter first and turned to see that Debbie had been sidetracked by a display of sock yarns.

"What is it about fabric and yarn that makes a shop like this so inviting?" Debbie asked Bonnie when she'd pulled herself away and joined Janet.

"The possibility of beautiful things to come," Bonnie said.

"That's the way I feel when I drool over a new cookbook." Janet laughed. "We have two questions for you. The first one's about the reproduction flour sacking material Kim Smith at the museum hoped you could track down. Have you had any luck?"

"Didn't Kim tell you?" Bonnie asked. "I found something very close to that darling apron's fabric—" She slapped a hand over her mouth, wide eyes darting between Janet and Debbie. She dropped her hand and said, "Kim asked me to keep it secret. It was supposed to be a surprise." She looked so annoyed with herself that Janet wanted to hug her.

"Then forget we even asked," Debbie said. "Surprise covers a lot of beautiful possibilities, so nothing's been spoiled, and we won't tell Kim."

"Speaking of beautiful." Janet took the scarf out and showed it to Bonnie. "Do you think any of this yarn came from here?"

"May I?" Bonnie took the scarf and held it up to see the full length and saw the tag pinned to it. "One of the anonymous hats. How fun!"

"Do you know who the knitter is?" Janet asked eagerly.

"I wish I did." Bonnie thought for a moment. "In September I had my annual 'Summer's Ending, Let's Get Ready for Winter Sale,' and I added any skein of yarn that was the last of a color. I remember that a volunteer from Faith Community Church bought all the single skeins of novelty yarn, and all the bright and unusual colors. She said she's mentoring a knitting group for some teens at the church. Does that help?"

"It might be the clue we need," Janet said. "Thanks!"

"Now I feel like my childhood heroine." Bonnie's eyes glittered. "Nancy Drew."

CHAPTER THIRTEEN

I've gotten behind in this journal. I haven't written yet about the trip home when I took Theo to meet Gran and Grandad. It went quite well. I'm teasing. The visit went stupendously well. Gran took me aside, before we left, and told me that she and Grandad like Theo very much. I told her that Theo has started coming to church with me. She said she saw a tear in Grandad's eye because he sees how much Theo and I love each other.

All of that is preamble for what happened after church today—Theo asked me to marry him, and I said yes!

By rights, Theo should have spoken to Grandad first. To fix that, we borrowed Mr. Lightwood's car, the Green Chariot, and drove to Steubenville so Theo could properly ask Grandad's permission. Dee had a knowing look in her eye when she saw us off, but if she's caught on to what we're up to she's playing along. She's a good friend.

On the way to Steubenville, Theo said he was a big ball of nerves but that it wouldn't stop him talking to Grandad. I gave him a kiss for bravery and told him to pay no mind to Grandad's stern look. That's just Grandad for you.

Grandad took Theo into the sitting room. Gran and I pretended to be calm. Gran kept muttering "Och, dearie me." When Theo and Grandad emerged from the sitting room, Gran and I both saw a tear in Grandad's eye. The old softy. That sent Gran over the edge and she was "greetin' like a bairn." That's how she says "crying like a baby." One look at her and I was greetin' too.

After many hugs, we drove back to Dennison, and I told Theo I would like to do something brave too. I would like to ask his mother's permission to marry her son. He liked the idea. He said his mother might think it was a little odd but that she'd put up with a lot of things that were more than a little bit odd from Dee over the years, so she'd had practice. We parked the Green Chariot. He gave me a kiss for bravery, and his mother met me at the door with hugs and tears because

Dee had spilled the beans. Dee was crying too, and I forgave her immediately.

We're planning a spring wedding in Steubenville when the flowers are blooming. I've always liked the rhyme about a bride needing "something old, something new, something borrowed, something blue, and a sixpence in her shoe." Gran says she's been saving a sixpence for me. Maybe I'll carry this diary in my handbag at the wedding for my something blue.

Mrs. Bartlett says she's pleased as punch about the wedding.

November 3, 1941

It was all I could do to concentrate at work today. I straightened my back, though, and pulled my weight, so no one could accuse me of daydreaming or shirking my duties. Lunch is another story. I stared off into space for a while (probably looking like a lovesick cow). Then I practiced writing my name-to-be. Mrs. Theodore Lightwood. Mrs. Theo Lightwood. Joyce Terrell Lightwood. Joyce Lightwood. I'm over the moon and as silly as a schoolgirl. I'm already thinking of names for our children.

November 4, 1941

Gran called me on the telephone. Long distance! She wants to start planning my wedding dress. She's sending sketches. Grandad took the telephone and said he'd forgotten to ask Theo an important question. Does he like to fish? I told him I would find out, and asked him if the answer is no, should I call the whole thing off? He said he'd trust my judgment on that.

CHAPTER FOURTEEN

"I didn't expect to be going back to high school twice in less than a week," Debbie said as she and Janet left the shop.

"Do you feel like you're in a time warp?" Janet asked as she drove them north out of Uhrichsville to the high school.

"Not really. I might if we were going to the old building where you and I graduated. When did this new one open?"

"In 2001," Janet said. "Long enough ago that it isn't so new anymore. How does that make you feel?"

"It's a basic fact of life," Debbie said. "Every single day not a single one of us is as new as we were the day before."

"Just a day wiser."

"Definitely wiser," Debbie said.

They parked in the visitors' lot in front of the school. As they entered the front doors, Janet made Debbie laugh by whispering, "Make sure you have your hall pass ready." They stopped in the office to sign in, and then Janet led the way to the auditorium. They entered at the back of the room with a view of the stage, where half a dozen students sat or stood as they read through their lines.

"Nice space," Debbie said, nodding approvingly. "A Goldilocks auditorium—just the right size. Is that Courtney sitting down front?"

"If it isn't, she might be backstage. She knows to be on the look-out for us. Let's go down there."

A sloping aisle led them between rows of red auditorium seats. They slipped into the front row next to a woman about their age with hair very nearly like Janet's own—shoulder-length and blond. The woman glanced at them with a smile, looked at the script in her hand, then held up five fingers, mouthing *five minutes*.

Janet sat back and enjoyed listening to the young actors attempting broad New York accents. The actors reached the end of a scene and looked toward the woman next to Janet.

"Excellent job, cast," the woman called. "Take a break and grab something to eat or drink."

"Can't we do both?" one of the students asked to laughter from the others.

"As long as you're back on stage and ready in ten minutes, I don't care if you take a nap. Set your timers. No slackers."

"What do you do if they aren't ready in ten minutes?" Janet asked.

"I've never had to find out. Aren't I lucky? Hi, I'm Courtney. Are you Janet?"

"Yes, and this is Debbie Albright."

Courtney pointed at them. "The women behind the Whistle Stop Café?" They nodded and she said, "Fantastic! I love seeing local places come alive. It's like seeing these kids put in the work and bring a play to life."

"That sounds like something Nellie Lightwood used to say in English class way back when," Janet said.

"She must have been a wonderful teacher. I wish I'd lived here when I was in high school," Courtney said. "I feel incredibly blessed to have known her, though."

"How long did she volunteer for you?" Debbie asked.

"I've only been teaching at Claymont High for two years. I taught special ed at the middle school for nine years before that. I inherited the treasure that was Nellie from the previous theater teacher. Come backstage, and I'll show you what she did for us."

They climbed a short flight of stairs to the stage and followed Courtney through the wings to a door. It led to a hall adjoining the back of the theater with doors along the opposite side.

Courtney indicated the open door across from them. "This is our technical theater workshop where we build the sets. There isn't much going on with that this week. But next week construction will be in full swing, and the sweet smells of sawdust and paint will follow us wherever we go." She walked down the hall to a door with an official-looking sign that said COSTUMES. Someone had painted NELLIE's above the sign, and below they'd painted a monarch butterfly. "The students loved Nellie," Courtney said. "This room and the next one were her domain."

Nellie's domain proved to be a classroom that had metamorphosed like a caterpillar into a butterfly. Tall metal cabinets lined the walls, and rows of racks, holding clothes and costumes of every description, filled the rest of the room.

"The cupboards contain shoes, hats, spectacles, beards, and every incidental you can think of," Courtney said. "We're prepared for ancient Greek dramas all the way up to plays written yesterday."

"Thanks to Nellie?" Janet asked.

"Mostly. Collecting for our plays was her passion. Her mission. Come see what's next door."

This door, labeled PROPS, had the same hand-painted additions as the costume room. Courtney opened it into a room also lined with metal cupboards but displaying a jigsaw puzzle of furniture, architectural elements, and a small nursery of trees and plants.

"Where did Nellie find a palm tree?" Janet marveled.

"Whenever I asked her about something she brought in," Courtney said, "she'd wave a hand like it was nothing at all to find a suit of armor kicking around somewhere."

"*Did* she find a suit of armor?" Debbie asked.

"No, but not for lack of trying, I'm sure." Courtney opened one of the metal cabinets. "Candlesticks, candelabras, potted plants, crystal bowls. Do you know how many theater teachers spend their own money tracking down stuff like this? Not to mention the time it takes, often on weekends. Nellie's passing was a tremendous loss to our program."

"It's all amazing," Janet said. "And it explains some of what we've heard about Nellie from her niece. She's been cleaning out Nellie's house." Janet told Courtney about the trunk Dawn took first to the *Days of Yesteryear* television show and then gave to the museum. When Janet described the clothes and the wedding dress, Courtney's interest visibly quickened.

"We started plans for this spring's musical more than a year ago," Courtney said. "I told you it's *Guys and Dolls*, right?"

Janet nodded.

"So, I wonder if Nellie meant those clothes for us. They're the right period, and there's even a wedding scene in the play."

"That could be," Debbie said, "but there were other things in it besides clothes."

"Recipes, for instance," Janet said, "and an apron that isn't in any shape to be used as a costume."

"Pieces from an unfinished quilt too," Debbie said. "Items that might indicate a personal connection between Nellie and the trunk. It's a long shot, but we wondered if she ever spoke about it with you?"

"She wouldn't discuss her foraging trips," Courtney said. "That's what she called them. But, from the description of the clothes, it just makes sense that she meant them for me. I mean"—she gave a little laugh—"for the theater department."

Janet wondered why Courtney's laugh sounded nervous, possibly the nervous laughter of someone bending the truth.

"I'm right, don't you think?" Courtney asked. "Oh, you're about to lose your hat."

Janet saw that the hat was spilling out of the bag and tucked it back in. As she did, she looked up. A girl in the open doorway briefly met her eyes then ducked and scurried away. Janet wondered if she'd been listening to their conversation. Even if she had been, did it matter?

"So, the trunk and the clothes?" Courtney's eyes darted from Janet to Debbie.

"We can't be sure who they were meant for just yet," Janet said carefully.

"And we wouldn't make that decision," Debbie added. "Kim Smith will make that call, since it all belongs to the museum for now. But thanks for seeing us. Good luck with the play."

On their way out of the building, after signing out in the office, Janet thought she saw the same girl again, watching them then pulling back around a corner.

Kim was just saying goodbye and hanging up the phone when Janet and Debbie appeared in her office doorway, ready to report on their visit to the high school. Kim seemed harried, as though she had a million things on her museum-director mind.

"Hold that thought," Janet said. "I'll be right back. Snacks to the rescue."

"Hurry," Debbie said. "I'll hold her hand until you return."

"You two," Kim said with a laugh. "You're just what I need right now."

Janet hurried to the café, grabbed three of the day's leftover muffins, and went back to Kim's office. "Sorry, no coffee, but muffins are known lifesavers. You're not often in a tizzy, Kim. What's up?"

"It's the wedding dress," Kim said. "Word of our mystery has spread faster and farther than we realized it would."

Janet handed the muffins around and sank into a chair. "Is this bad news?"

"More like exhausting news," Kim said. "Let me apply the muffin where it's needed most and I'll tell you." After eating the last crumb with a happy sigh, Kim told them that she'd had several phone calls from people offering to buy the wedding dress, sight unseen, including one from Columbus.

"Uh-oh," Debbie said. "Fruits of our questions at the basketball game?"

"We didn't keep it quiet," Janet said. "Sorry, Kim."

"It's fine," Kim said. "Word was bound to spread. I think these are people after a bargain. They probably hope to resell the dress for a mint."

"But isn't that kind of odd?" Janet asked. "How often do people call and ask to buy something that belongs to a museum?"

"It hasn't happened to me before," Kim admitted. "But the dress hasn't been cataloged into our collection, and people don't necessarily know the nitty-gritty of running a museum. Some people arrive here and say they are amazed that we're a 'real' museum, which they see as a compliment." Kim smiled. "I do too, actually."

"Because Dawn gave the dress to the museum, the museum is free to dispose of it however it sees fit, right?" Debbie asked.

"That's what Dawn agreed to when she left the trunk here," Kim said.

"Then if the dress is worth something, the museum can sell it after the fashion show," Debbie pointed out. "Put the money into the museum's discretionary fund, if there is one, or add it to the budget's line item for monetary gifts."

"An option," Kim said.

"And in the meantime, there isn't really anything to worry about, is there?" Debbie asked. "The calls are a nuisance, I'm sure, but the dress is here, and it's safe."

"Safe." Janet looked at her friends, wondering if she should voice a worry growing in the back of her mind. Her friends studied her face.

"What?" Debbie asked.

"That wart I have," Janet said. "You know the one. The worry wart."

"Your worries are our worries," Kim said. "Spill."

Janet told her about their visit to Claymont High and what they learned about Nellie's volunteer work. "I love that Nellie had such a comfortable relationship with the students," she said.

"And a passion for finding what they needed," Debbie added. "It paints a different picture of her. In front of our eyes she transformed from a hoarder into a beloved, self-appointed prop manager."

"What a lovely way to spend her retirement," Kim said. "So what's the worry?"

"Given this interest in the dress," Janet said, "what if Courtney knows more about the trunk, the clothes, and especially the dress than she said? She made a point of telling us that she and Nellie didn't talk about where she found what she donated to the school. That Nellie *wouldn't* tell her. What if that isn't true? What if Nellie told Courtney about the wedding dress, and Courtney knows it has resale value?" Far from feeling better, Janet felt worse for spilling her worry about Courtney.

"But surely that dress isn't worth all that much. It isn't like it's by a famous designer or anything. I checked, and there's no label or other telltale signs it was couture," Kim said. "Do you have any reason to believe Courtney knew about it?"

"Maybe," Debbie said. "It might have been a slip of the tongue, but when Courtney said she felt sure Nellie meant to donate the clothes, including the wedding dress, she didn't say 'to the theater department.' She said, 'to me.' She corrected herself, but first she did say 'to me.'"

"Frankly, she seemed nervous," Janet said.

"She might just be so invested in the theater department that it's part of her," Kim said. "I'm sure I slip like that with the museum. And you two are the Whistle Stop Café."

It was a good point, Janet thought.

"She also mentioned the problem many theater teachers have," Debbie said. "That they end up using their own money for props and costumes."

"And the time it takes to find what they need," Janet added.

"Let's take note of her eagerness to have the clothes," Kim said. "But if you planned to donate a trunk of clothes to the school, would you push it to the back of an attic crawl space where it would be inconvenient to drag back out, let alone get it out of the house?"

"That sounds like a point for our side," Debbie said.

"It makes sense, and maybe Courtney will accept that," Janet said. "And no, we don't have a concrete reason to believe she's after the wedding dress. But a piece of advice Nellie gave us, back in the day, was to always leave a margin for the unexpected. I don't know if we need a margin, but where the wedding dress is concerned, let's at least keep an eye out for anything unusual."

"Courtney's slips," Debbie said.

"The phone calls from people who want to buy it," Kim groaned.

"And anything else that doesn't quite fit," Janet finished.

Janet slid a taco casserole into the oven for supper and set the timer. She'd already prepared a green salad and put it in the fridge. Now she had twenty-five minutes before the casserole came out and about thirty before Ian got home. She sat at the kitchen table and opened her laptop. She finally had the time to write down the questions they'd been batting back and forth without giving them serious thought. She opened a document and created a bulleted list.

- *Can we identify the author of the note in the wedding dress pocket by comparing it to the other examples of handwriting in the trunk?*
- *Where did Nellie find the quilt squares and the recipe box?*
- *Is Courtney after the wedding dress? For the school or for herself?*
- *Does the teen knitting group teacher know who the anonymous knitter is?*
- *What information would we still like from Dawn?*
- *What was the intruder after at Nellie's?*
- *Why did Nellie start calling her mother Thelma, shortly after Thelma died? How can we find that out? Do we need to?*

Ranger jumped into Janet's lap. She stroked him between his ears. "We *don't* need to know why she switched from 'Mama' to 'Thelma.' It's part of the deeper story of Nellie, though, and her story is pulling me in. There are so many questions, Ranger, and I can't help feeling sad that we may never know all the answers."

"Did you have a good day?" Ian asked after taking a bite and complimenting Janet on the taco casserole.

"I did. Interesting too, starting first thing when I found one of the anonymous hats sitting on a bench at the depot."

"Did you take it with you or leave it?"

"Are you kidding? I grabbed it before anyone else came along," Janet said, "and I have plans to regift it."

"I like it when you look pleased with yourself like that." Ian took seconds of the casserole and a smaller second helping of salad. "I also like this casserole. Oh, but I already said that, didn't I?"

Janet laughed. "I like it when you enjoy a dish so much you forget you've already said how good it is. Debbie and I went to the high school and met the theater teacher, Courtney McCampbell. She showed us what Nellie had done for them as a volunteer." She described the costume and props rooms for Ian.

"That's delightful," Ian said. "Think of what that did for Nellie too. It probably gave her real joy and purpose in her retirement."

"So a question for you with your chief hat on. Have you ever heard anything concerning Courtney McCampbell officially? If you can say."

"She's never come to my attention."

"Good," Janet said. "That's good."

"Should she?"

"I doubt it," Janet said. "You know me and my active imagination. *Over*active sometimes."

Ian tipped his head and looked at her. "That's just it. I do know you. You do have an active imagination but in my experience it isn't unwarranted. You have good radar about these things."

"But I think I'm probably tilting at windmills in this case," Janet said. "There, 'tilting at windmills.' That's from *Don Quixote*, something I read for extra credit to please Nellie Lightwood. So, no, I don't think there's any need for Courtney to come to your attention. I hope."

CHAPTER FIFTEEN

Joyce Terrell's Diary
December 7, 1941

The news today is horrible. Shocking and horrible.
Mrs. Bartlett and I were listening to the radio this
afternoon, and I was madly trying to finish Grandad's
scarf for Christmas—like the one I knitted for Theo—
when the program was interrupted with a bulletin.
Japan has attacked our islands of Hawaii! They
bombed Honolulu and Pearl Harbor, killing so many
sailors and soldiers and wounding so many more.
More reports came in throughout the afternoon and
evening—there were attacks on other islands in the
Pacific and on the Philippine Islands too. Looking at
Grandad's scarf tonight, I saw where I dropped a couple
of stitches. I know exactly when that happened—when

that first report came over the radio. I will leave the mistake. This day should never be forgotten.

December 8, 1941

Our country is at war. It's hard to believe. On the radio tonight, President Roosevelt said, "Yesterday, December 7, 1941, is a date which will live in infamy." He has asked Congress to declare war on the Empire of Japan. He said that our people, our territory, and our interests are in grave danger. I wanted to cry. Mrs. Bartlett did cry and put her apron over her face. She lost her husband in the Great War. The war that was supposed to end all of them. Mr. Roosevelt said that with our unbounding determination we will gain the inevitable triumph—so help us God. I remember what he said in his Fireside Chat back in September when the Nazi submarine fired on one of our destroyers. From now on I will end my bedtime prayers with those words—"Yours in prayer for divine help and guidance."

December 11, 1941

More awful news. Germany and Italy have declared war on us. On the United States. Dee broke down over lunch. She would only say "It's been hard to sleep. Sometimes it's hard to breathe," and looked at me with sad, hollow eyes.

December 12, 1941

The bad news does not stop. I now know why Dee finds it hard to breathe. My heart is finding it hard to continue beating, and I feel unbearably selfish saying that. Theo enlisted. He's been inducted and told to report for basic training Monday, January 5th. He told me when he walked me home from work. I told him that I'm very proud of him. When I got home I came up to my room and cried.

December 15, 1941

I called Gran. She gave me a good bucking up. She told me what a good, patriotic man I'm marrying. That we will do our part, here at home too. I told her that Theo and I have decided to push our wedding date up to January 3rd, to marry before he leaves for basic training the next day. I held back my tears for the beautiful spring wedding I'd imagined. Gran could hear them in my voice, though, and she reminded me that she and Grandad came through the first war. "War is not for greetin'," she said. "It's time for getting down to the business at hand."

Then I had to laugh. The business she has in mind is finding the time to finish the wedding dress during a busy holiday season.

Flowers won't be blooming for our wedding, and snow might be flying, but Theo and I have our faith, and love, and I know that all will be well.

CHAPTER SIXTEEN

*J*anet sang to herself as she baked the next morning. Her spirit felt lighter after making her list of questions, and lighter still after she'd sent the questions to Debbie and Kim. *A worry shared is a worry halved,* she thought. Or, in this case, reduced by two-thirds. When she ran out of words to sing, she switched to humming.

"Good morning, friend," she called when Debbie arrived.

"Good morning yourself. What's that you're humming? 'Wait Till the Sun Shines, Nellie?'"

"So it is. I hadn't even thought. Seems appropriate, doesn't it?"

"It's so hopeful. A perfect way to start the day." Debbie disappeared into the office and came out tying on an apron. The bib had a picture of a steaming cup of coffee under the words I COULD GIVE UP COFFEE, BUT I'M NO QUITTER. "The questions you sent last night were succinct and to the point."

"Good. Making the list and getting it all out of my head helped me sleep better. I asked Ian if he's ever heard anything about Courtney officially."

"Yeah? Has he?"

"No, but really, what was I thinking? That she's a serial co-opter of other people's stuff so she can make money selling it?"

"That might be the definition of burglar," Debbie said. "Huh. I meant that as a joke, but we do have questions about an intruder."

"At Nellie's house." Janet plopped onto a stool. "Oh brother. I'd forgotten about that."

Debbie nodded. "If it's any consolation, I asked Greg if he's ever heard any scuttlebutt about Courtney around the school or around town. He said he knows who she is, but he's only ever heard how hard she works and how much the students like her."

"I liked her too."

"Same." Debbie put her hand on Janet's shoulder. "When we wondered about Dawn being in cahoots with the intruder, you calmed us down by saying we shouldn't be uncharitable toward someone we don't know. Let's give that grace to Courtney too."

"But—" Janet started to say.

"But." Debbie held up a finger. "Being charitable doesn't mean turning a blind eye or deaf ear. We'll keep those open. Now, you practice your superpower and bake, and I'll go get us opened up for a cheerful, friendly day. Oh, and did you know it's snowing?"

"To that I say let it snow. But not too much. Thanks, partner." Janet went back to humming. She decided to add dream bars to the day's menu and make the extras they'd need for the fashion show.

When Paulette arrived for her shift, she told them the forecast was calling for the snow to taper off by noon. "Only for the afternoon, though. Round two starts this evening and should continue overnight. They're saying we can expect anywhere from 'not much' to 'oh my aching back, that was more than I needed to shovel.' People are already stripping the grocery shelves of milk and bread."

"Stocking up on milk and bread is so old hat," Debbie said. "If they're smart, they'll come in here and stock up on pastries."

The snow didn't taper off. It picked up right along with business at lunchtime, and neither the snow nor the stream of hungry customers slowed by the usual end of lunch rush.

"I think you got your wish about the pastries," Janet said as she brought another tray of double chocolate muffins out to the bakery case. "It's like we're having a party." She straightened the last few scones on the tray next to the muffins, and when she stood up she was surprised to see who Paulette was waiting on—the high school girl who'd scurried away from the props room door and the corner by the school office the day before.

The girl ordered a cup of decaf coffee and one of the double chocolate muffins. She paid, took the coffee and muffin, and sat at a table by the windows.

Janet waited on the next few customers while Paulette quickly wiped down tables. When Janet had a moment to breathe, the girl was watching her. Janet felt sure she recognized the signs of someone who wanted to say something. She smiled at the girl and called, "Can I get you a refill on the coffee?"

The girl hesitated and then started toward the counter with her cup. Just then a woman with her phone to her ear burst through the door. She stopped, blocking the girl's path, her exuberant voice attracting everyone's attention. "The whole town is *too* adorable," she crowed into her phone. "The downtown, the depot, the Whistle Stop Café. Isn't the name just too much?" She twirled for a better look at the whole café, making the girl back up, and then planted herself and her things at the counter, somehow taking up as much room as three people. "I'm in the café now, and it is cute, cute, cute. The delicious smells! I should hang up and order something, though, and then I have an appointment with the museum director. I know! How exciting is that? Talk to you later." She pocketed her phone and beamed at Janet.

"If you don't mind," Janet said, "I think the young woman was ahead of you."

The woman whirled around, but the girl shook her head. "You sure?" the woman asked. The girl nodded.

"What can I get you then?" Janet asked. "Coffee?"

"Super. And one of something good from your case. Do you think they're fresh? Are they made locally? Hang on, let me take a look." She slid over to look in the bakery case. "Let's do the coffee and an orange-cranberry muffin. Make the coffee large in case the muffin's dry." She watched Janet pouring the coffee. "I'm waiting for an appointment with Kim Smith at the museum. Do you know if she's usually on time for appointments?"

"I'm sure she is," Janet said, "unless something comes up." She set a muffin on a plate and slid it across the counter. "Can I get you anything else?"

The woman was on her phone again.

People falling in love with Dennison as a whole, and especially with the café, always gave Janet a boost. The boost, this time, sagged a bit when she saw that the girl was gone. Janet went to the windows but didn't see her anywhere. She did spot Dawn, in a swirl of snow. Janet remembered how Dawn liked her coffee and had a cup ready for her when she came through the door, stamping snow from her shoes. Dawn took the coffee cup from her, wrapping red hands around it. She buried her nose in the steam then looked accusingly at a purse sitting on the counter in front of an unoccupied stool.

"It's hers," Janet said quietly with a little nod toward the woman on the phone. She nudged the purse closer to the woman's elbow, and Dawn sat. "Can I get you something to go with the coffee?"

Dawn hadn't, so far, smiled or said a word. "Grilled cheese and vegetable soup."

"Coming right up," Debbie said. She touched Janet's shoulder. "Your turn for a breather."

Gratefully, Janet poured herself a cup of coffee and watched Dawn blow her cheeks out as if she'd just run a tight race. "We've learned quite a bit about the quilt squares that were in the trunk, Dawn."

"How?" Dawn asked.

"By asking questions and following up on leads. It's a fascinating story."

"If you say so."

"We don't have anything on the wedding dress yet."

"You know," Dawn said, peering at Janet through narrowed eyes, "when I gave the trunk to the museum, I didn't expect people to be asking questions about it all over town." She put her coffee cup down. "I'm not sure it's a good idea either. I'm surprised you do."

"Dawn, we—"

Dawn spoke over Janet. "If you're telling anyone who asks that the trunk came from Nellie's house, you might as well put an ad in the paper announcing the house is empty. Because when you tell *those* people, you're also telling all their relatives and friends and anyone they happen to meet in the grocery store. That might be why someone broke into the house. Did you stop to think of that?"

Janet felt a blush warming her cheeks. She *hadn't* thought of that, except… "But Dawn, we opened the trunk Sunday afternoon. The break-in was the next morning, and you're the only person we talked to about the trunk before that."

The woman sitting next to Dawn set her phone down and leaned on her elbow, drinking in the drama. Janet moved to the end of the counter away from the woman. Dawn swiveled on her stool to keep her eyes on Janet, turning her back to the woman.

"Has it happened again?" Janet asked quietly.

"No. Sorry I bit your head off. You're right, but when I came in here I smelled the same scent I smelled in the house. It brought the whole thing back to me." Dawn's eyes narrowed further.

Janet, palms raised, took a step back. "The only scent I'm wearing is fresh-baked pastries with overtones of coffee and hints of lunch." That didn't raise a smile. She tried to think who'd been in the café when Dawn walked in, but it was too hard to say. Customers had been coming and going since eleven. Even now most of the tables were occupied. Then when she'd given Dawn the cup of coffee, Dawn had buried her nose in it. "You described it as a delicate scent. A good whiff of coffee can overpower other smells for me. Did you still smell the scent after I handed the cup to you?"

Dawn pursed her lips and thought then shrugged. The woman next to her checked the time and left. Debbie brought Dawn's soup and sandwich, and that finally brought a smile. "This is a much better smell," Dawn said. "Thank you." She took a bite of the sandwich, closing her eyes for a moment. "I love a good grilled cheese." She lifted her coffee cup. "And a good cup of coffee. You do both of them right."

"Then let me get you a refill," Janet said.

Dawn seemed to relax. Business slowed. The snow didn't.

Paulette cleaned tables again then said she'd be on her way. "I know it's a bit early," she said. "Something tells me it's a good idea to get home and off the roads."

"Go, go," Debbie said.

"What's our snow day policy?" Paulette asked.

Janet and Debbie looked at each other.

Paulette laughed. "No worries. Make something up and let me know."

Debbie put a dream bar on a plate and set it in front of Dawn.

Dawn cracked another smile. "Your unfailing good humor, in addition to your good food, goes a long way toward taming my foul mood."

"Food and friendship," Janet said. "They're simple gifts."

Dawn closed her eyes again. "I'm not sure I deserve them," she whispered.

More customers came in. "I'll get them," Debbie said quietly. "You sit with Dawn."

Janet put a dream bar on a second plate and took the stool next to Dawn. "I love these things," she said. "It's my grandmother's recipe. I'd forgotten all about it until I found it in the recipe box in the trunk. I didn't tell you that we've found out more about Nellie and the stuff she collected." She told Dawn about Nellie's volunteer work.

"So you've been asking even more questions." Dawn sounded on edge again. "And it turns out that Nellie had friends. My husband and I didn't know that. All we knew about her was what we thought we saw—a whiffy old woman. Whiffy is what we say in my family when someone isn't all there."

"From what I've been hearing, she was a wonderful and unusual person," Janet said. "She did a wonderful thing for me back in high school. She wrote a recommendation that got me a college scholarship. That meant the world to me."

"You thanked her, of course."

"With a proper thank-you letter. Then I went on with my life, and now I regret not thinking about her all these years. You don't live here. I *do* live in this town, which isn't all that big, and I managed to completely lose track of her. It's no good to beat ourselves up with regrets, but I do regret that."

"Nellie had a massive stroke before she died."

"I didn't know that. See what I mean about losing track?"

"I came to see her," Dawn said. "She seemed to understand what I said, but she couldn't make herself understood."

"So sad," Janet said.

"Heartbreaking, and obviously frustrating to her. She mostly sat and said nothing. My husband would have been Nellie's executor. That fell to me when he passed. When I assured her the house and everything would be taken care of, she tried to say something but I couldn't understand. She tried so hard, but it made no sense. And then she was gone. It wasn't quite sudden death, but sudden enough."

"That's always a horrible shock," Janet said. "I'm so sorry."

"Puppy jump," Dawn said.

"I'm sorry?"

"That's one of the things Nellie said after the stroke. Clear as day. When I asked her what she meant, she tried again. She said, 'dinette set,' then 'pepper pot,' then 'pilot junk.' Then she gave up.

The nurse told me the words might have no connection at all to what she was trying to say."

"Awful," Janet said.

Dawn pushed the cookie away and said nothing.

"The quilt blocks have a connection to your husband's family. Thelma made one of them. Kim would be happy to give them to you if you'd like to have them."

"I'm not interested in collecting anything," Dawn said. "I've become a firm believer in a clutter-free home."

"Wouldn't you at least like the one with their great-grandmother's name for your children?" Janet asked.

"They have no real connection to Dennison. No real connection to Nellie. They're not into quilting either. They're busy young professionals. You know the type."

"I used to *be* the type," Debbie said as she cleared away Dawn's dishes. "I'll put this dream bar in a bag for you.

"The blocks are in good condition," Janet said. "They might be worth some money. Kim thinks the fabrics are vintage flour sacking."

Dawn shook her head. "I actually checked. Bundles of 1930- and 1940-era quilt blocks go for twenty-five or thirty dollars, even with embroidered signatures. If the blocks have been sewn together into a quilt top—pieced—is that the term?"

"It is," Janet said.

"Pieced vintage quilt tops are listed for several hundred dollars. Some even more. But they're only worth that if someone will pay that much for them. It's a moot point anyway. These are just the blocks. They are lovely, but if the museum wants to keep them or make a little money off them, I'm all for it."

Janet nodded. "Thanks for telling me about Nellie."

"Her struggle to get the words out, to make me understand, still haunts me." Dawn stood to go. "The sad thing is, I didn't take the time to understand her when I had the chance, before the stroke."

Janet watched Dawn go back out into the blowing snow. "I hope she's going to be okay."

"Problems?" Debbie asked.

Janet told her about Nellie's stroke.

"Poor Nellie," Debbie said. "So eloquent as a teacher and then not able to make herself understood. She must have felt very far away from everyone and everything."

"And now I won't be able to stop wondering if what she was trying to say would have given us a clue or an answer about the wedding dress."

"That seems pretty far-fetched," Debbie said. "We don't even know if she knew it was in the trunk."

"Sadly, it does seem far-fetched. Like so many of the clues I think I've found. Which might not turn out to be clues at all."

CHAPTER SEVENTEEN

*J*anet stayed late to help Debbie clean up after their bonanza of customers. Before they could start, their phones buzzed with simultaneous texts from Kim.

WILL YOU COME OVER? SOMEONE IS HERE ABOUT THE WEDDING DRESS.

Debbie had just locked the door behind the last happy customer. She raised her eyebrows at Janet. "See Kim first, then clean up?"

"Let's go."

They hurried through the museum lobby and stopped outside Kim's closed office door.

"Maybe they're in the workroom," Debbie said.

Janet stepped closer to the door and heard voices. "Just a closed-door meeting, I guess. I wonder why?" She knocked.

"Come on in," a woman's voice called.

Debbie caught Janet's arm. "That's not Kim. Why is someone else asking us in?"

"No idea. She sounded familiar, though. Come on. We may as well see what's up." Janet opened the door far enough to look around the edge. "Kim?"

Kim sat behind her desk wearing a smile that wasn't one of her most convincing. Sitting in one of the guest chairs in front of the desk, but twisted around so she could grin at Janet, was the woman who'd come into the café speaking loudly into her phone. Janet opened the door the rest of the way, and Kim waved them in, her smile warming into something that looked a bit like relief.

"Janet Shaw and Debbie Albright, I'd like you to meet—"

"Renee Peterson," the woman said to a quickly subdued eye roll, behind her back, from Kim. "I love, love, love your cute café. Come sit down. Kim rustled up an extra chair so all four of us can chat." She patted the seat closest to her.

"Thanks," Debbie said.

"But close the door. I feel like this is a big secret."

"Renee thinks the wedding dress might belong to her family," Kim said.

"I don't *think*, Kim, and it isn't *might*. I'm sure it belongs to my family." Renee put her hand on her heart. "I feel it right here. I came all the way from Columbus, and with the way the snow was coming down, maybe I shouldn't have. I'm glad it's stopped, but please don't let me go home empty-handed."

"How did you hear about the dress?" Janet asked.

"A friend right here in Dennison told me. Am I right that you haven't discovered anything about the wedding dress yet?"

"We haven't," Debbie said. "What can you tell us about it?"

"First let me say that I doubt you will discover anything at all about it. That's because I'm the last person who knows the real story."

"When I told Renee I'd like you to hear her story too, she wouldn't even give me a teaser without you two," Kim said.

Renee laughed. "Thanks for waiting, Kim. It's such a romantic story. A tale, really. I didn't want you to miss it. Picture this—my

Nanny Mona, engaged to her handsome soldier, waiting for him to return from the war. She expected him in May, and they were to be married in June, the most romantic month. Only, he didn't return, and the dress went unworn, until—" She paused dramatically, hand to her heart again. "Two whole years later he reappeared. Here's what happened. Days before shipping for home, his company was ambushed. He was seriously wounded, a terrible head injury." Her hand moved dramatically to her head. "He ended up at Walter Reed Army Medical Center. When he was eventually released, he went home to live with his parents. Now for the most tragic part. As sometimes happens with head injuries, he'd lost his memory. His parents hadn't known he was engaged, and now he didn't either." Renee closed her eyes and shook her head.

"Memories do sometimes recover, though, and his slowly, slowly came back. He remembered his dear Mona and knew he had to find her. And he did. He found where she lived, took a deep breath, and knocked on her door. She opened it, and when she saw him there with a dozen red roses, she fainted and fell into his arms. They married a month later. But she didn't wear the beautiful dress she'd bought two years earlier. It still hung in her closet, but Nanny Mona told me more than once, that had been a different time, a different place, and now they were different people. 'But not so different, Renee,' she'd say at the end of her story, 'not so different that we didn't have a lovely, loving life together.'"

"Did you ever see the dress?" Kim asked.

"No! She always told me it was safely put away. I looked for it after she died but never found it. Until now."

"Did your grandmother describe the dress?" Kim asked. "Was there anything special about it to distinguish it from another dress of the period?"

"You don't believe me?" Renee asked.

"I'm being careful, as I'm sure you want me to be, and as I have to be," Kim said. "Unless we know what your grandmother's dress looked like, there's no way to prove the one we have is hers. Anyone could come forward and claim it with a story. You see that, don't you?"

"Can I at least see the dress you have? I'm sure I'll recognize it."

"So she did describe it to you?" Janet asked.

"Yes. She had a picture of it too. May I see it now?"

"I can show you a picture of ours," Kim said. She tapped at her keyboard and turned her laptop around for Renee to see.

Renee stared at the laptop screen. "Oh my goodness. I'm sure that's it. It must be Nanny Mona's dress."

"If it is, we'll be happy to discuss reuniting you with it," Kim said. "Will you do me the favor of sending me the information you have about the dress? Why you think this particular one out of all the vintage wedding dresses there are in this area? Any photographs too, if you have them, and then I'll be in—"

"I can do better than that." Renee pulled a piece of paper from her purse. "I came prepared. It's all here, the whole story with names and dates. Except for the photograph." She handed the paper to Kim. "I need to dig through some boxes to find that. But I will. You can bet I will." She stood to go. "Thank you, Kim, so, so much for listening to me. It was great meeting you, Debbie and Janet." Renee turned at the door. "When do you think I'll hear from you, Kim?"

"I'll be in touch as soon as I see the picture."

To the door Renee closed behind her, Kim said, "I'll be in touch as soon as I see the picture *and* after a good bit of research."

"Do you doubt her story?" Janet asked.

"Not necessarily, but there are some pretty wide gaps. I'll be happier after I look into it. The story, as she told it, doesn't prove anything, and it doesn't matter whether I believe it or not."

"She knows the dress wasn't worn," Debbie said.

"We might have let that slip when we told people about it," Janet said.

"Or Dawn might have," Debbie said. "But Renee didn't say anything about the pocket."

"She might not know about it," Kim said. "It's amazing the secrets families are able to keep hidden, and the wedding dress was *literally* hidden. If Renee's to be believed, she's a romantic. Maybe Nanny Mona was too, and kept the pocket a secret to be discovered."

"Kim, what time was Renee's appointment?" Janet asked.

"Appointment?"

"She told whoever she was talking to on the phone, when she came into the café, that she had one. Then she asked me if you're on time for appointments."

Kim's lips pressed into a thin line.

"No appointment?" Janet asked. "Okay, I'm confused."

"You're confused, and I'm annoyed. Can you tell?" Kim asked. "Let's back up. When did she come into the café?"

Janet looked at Debbie. "About one o'clock?"

"Close enough," Debbie said.

"Let me guess," said Kim. "Renee came in loud and happy."

"*Gushing* is the word I would use," Debbie said. "I heard her, and I was in the kitchen."

"She asked for coffee then asked if the muffins are made locally and hoped they weren't too dry," Janet said.

"That's enough to put me off her right there," said Kim.

"Thank you. You're a good friend," Janet said. "In all fairness, it wasn't an unreasonable question. She was just asking out loud what a lot of people probably want to know."

"People who might think of a better way to find out. Like this. 'Ooh,'" Kim said in a high breathless voice, "'Those muffins look so good. Did someone bake them this morning?'"

"Renee might not be as cunning as you," Janet said. "After gushing her way through the door, she sat at the counter. When Dawn came in, she thought someone was already sitting next to Renee because Renee's purse was on the counter in front of the stool next to her. I slid Renee's purse over closer to her, and Dawn sat down."

"What were you and Dawn talking about?" Debbie asked. "Dawn got kind of intense, but that seems like her most frequent operating mode. And Renee found it interesting."

"Wow." Janet scrubbed her hands over her face. "I told her we'd learned the story behind the quilt squares but not the wedding dress. She said that asking questions around town was like putting an ad in the paper telling everyone Nellie's house is empty, and that might be why she had the intruder. I told her we'd only looked in the trunk the day before her break-in and hadn't asked any questions at that point. But do you remember the scent she smelled in the house after the intruder came in? Dawn said she smelled it again when she came into the café. I feel like a fool."

"Why?" Kim asked.

"Renee heard all that."

"But you didn't describe the dress, did you?" Kim asked.

"No."

"Or give out Nellie's address?" Debbie asked.

"No. Okay, that makes me feel better. Plus, Renee told the person on the phone about the appointment with you *before* Dawn came in."

"Isn't there something a little...too much about Renee?" Kim asked.

"Expressive," Debbie said. "That goes along with gushing. That could be acting, or it might just be her."

"Think about what she said before she told us her story," Janet said. "First she called it romantic, then a tale."

"A slip because she really was spinning a tale?" Kim asked. "Hmm."

"And if she didn't have an appointment with you," Janet continued, "why did she say she did? Right before she left the café, she looked at her phone, like she was checking the time, and then she rushed back out of the café. But that was easily an hour before you sent your text."

"So where did she go in between the café and the museum?" Debbie asked. "And why lie about having an appointment with you?"

"We should have asked who the friend was who told her about the dress," Janet said.

"I thought about asking," Kim said, "but couldn't think why we'd need to know."

"After the fact, I can for two reasons," Janet said. "One, it might be nice to know if this friend actually exists, and two, if the answer to that is yes, then we could ask this friend what she knows about Renee."

"That's the kind of awkward conversation I'd rather not have," Kim said. "Let's see what I find in conversation with databases first. The paper she gave me has her grandmother's and the fiancé's full names, so we might not need to know the friend's name. Now, Debbie, it's high time you try on the wedding dress. I set up a make-shift changing room in the workroom with a trifold screen."

Debbie bit her lip. "What if I split a seam?"

"I'll come with you," Janet said. "If it's the least bit tight we won't force it."

They went to the workroom, and Kim handed the dress to Debbie. "Here goes nothing," Debbie said. "I'll call you if I need help." She disappeared behind the screen.

"Have you found enough models?" Janet asked while she and Kim waited.

"I wouldn't mind one or two more, in case someone has to back out, but it's coming together. We're getting a great response too. Most of the tickets are sold, and the show is still a week and a half away."

"Exciting," Janet said. "I have dream bars in the freezer. We've placed our orders for everything else. Early next week I'll start on the rest of the menu items that can be made ahead."

From behind the screen, fabric rustled gently. "Debbie, how are you doing? Need help with the zipper?" Janet called.

"No, I'm fine," Debbie responded, her voice muffled. Janet pictured her speaking with the dress over her head. "It zips up the side, not the back, so I can manage." Her voice was clearer this time, like the dress had settled over her shoulders.

Janet was on pins and needles to see the beautiful garment worn by a real woman, as it was intended to be, rather than limp and lifeless on a hanger. She only hoped Debbie was not uncomfortable. Had she been insensitive when she pressed Debbie to model the dress, knowing that Debbie's fiancé, a soldier, had been killed in action before they could marry? And even though Debbie and Greg seemed to be enjoying each other's company, maybe matrimony wasn't their final destination. Had Debbie only agreed to wear the dress because the previous model had dropped out? It would be just like Debbie to be so selfless. She would talk to Debbie about it later, and if she needed to apologize, she would.

"Well, what do you think?" Preceded by another rustle of skirts, Debbie stepped around the screen and planted herself in front of Janet and Kim.

She was, in a word, breathtaking. The dress flattered her as if an expert seamstress had fitted it. Janet was momentarily speechless, and Kim must have been in the same state, because silence filled the workspace.

Debbie looked down, a bit uncertainly, and pulled up the skirts to her knees then held out one foot. "I admit these sneakers don't exactly say runway, but is it that bad?"

Kim found her voice first. "Debbie, you will be the star of the show, even if you wear pink bunny slippers and the world's most spectacular case of bedhead."

Debbie seemed to relax then smiled. "Janet? What's your opinion?"

A lump of emotion rose in Janet's throat. "You, my friend, are beautiful, inside and out."

Ian called as Janet was taking a package of ground beef from the freezer. "Sorry, love. I missed seeing that there's a budget meeting tonight."

"Your favorite thing. Lucky you."

"They bribed us by calling it a dinner meeting and brought in a mound of pulled pork sandwiches. I told them there needed to be brownies too, or they'd have to drag me through the door and tie me to a chair."

"See you later, tough guy," Janet said with a laugh, and disconnected. She looked at the package of ground beef in her hand, tossed it back into the freezer, and called Debbie. "Got anything going on tonight?"

"Greg and I were going out, but poor Julian went home early from school with a bug. So, our plans were canceled. It seemed like a good idea to avoid catching it and spreading it inadvertently at the café."

"Yikes."

Half an hour later, with a large pizza riding shotgun, Janet parked in Debbie's driveway. Debbie opened the door when Janet stepped onto the porch just as their phones buzzed.

"Kim," Debbie said, glancing at her phone "She's sending us an email." They went to the kitchen, where Janet put the pizza on the counter. "I'm texting back to see if she's still at the museum, if she's eaten, and if she's free to join us."

Yes, no, and yes, Kim sent.

While Debbie tapped out a long text in response, Janet pre-empted her and called Kim. "I'm at Debbie's, and I brought enough pizza to split three ways."

"Barry doesn't know the fun he misses when he works late," Kim said, referring to her husband. "The next knock on the door will be me. Five minutes, tops."

"She'll be here in five," Janet said.

"Show off," Debbie said with a laugh, deleting the half-finished text.

"Just the fastest speed dialer in the west." Janet blew on her phone, like a cowgirl blowing on the tip of her pistol, and slipped it into her pocket.

Over slices of a gut-buster pizza, an everything-but-the-kitchen-sink concoction, Kim told them what she'd discovered so far in her research.

"First, it occurred to me we never looked any further into what happened to Donna Collins after she and her family left town. I found her and her children—but not her husband—in the 1950 census for Bakersfield, California. Based on cemetery records, it appears that he died not long after they moved. Donna died in the '80s, and I didn't find anything of note about her kids. I'm not sure what I expected to find—some smoking gun about the quilt or the contents of the trunk, maybe. But it looks like a dead-end."

Janet shook her head. "Thanks, Kim, for picking up the slack in our investigation. I can't believe I didn't think to do even a little research into Donna. So what did you find out about Renee and her family?"

"Enough to put the kibosh on her claim to the dress. That's what I was going to email to you—a report of my findings. Do you want to read it?"

"As long as we let you take a bite once in a while, why don't you just tell us?" Janet asked.

"Also promise you won't eat my share while I'm telling you." Kim took her laptop from her satchel, logged on, and brought up her document. "Renee's grandmother, Mona, married Stuart Peterson in Dennison in 1955."

"Shall we call her that?" Debbie said. "Renee's grandmother? Or should we call her the woman Renee *claims* is her grandmother?"

"Good question," Kim said. "But no interruptions, please, and all will be revealed. Old phone books have a listing for Stuart and Mona Peterson on Gorley Street in Uhrichsville from 1955 to 1972. They were listed again, from 1982 until 1988, on Wilson Street in Dennison. According to her obituary, Mona died in 2003 in Columbus. It said that she and Stuart were married for forty-two years. He preceded her in death. She was survived by her son, Stuart Jr., and a granddaughter, Renee Peterson. Stuart's obituary, in 1997, tells briefly of his army service in the Korean War. Stuart, Jr. died in 2020, preceded in death by his wife in 2014."

"So Renee's story could be true," Janet said. "Good. I didn't like the idea of someone being so greedy they'd lie about a grandmother's wedding dress."

"On the other hand"—Kim looked over her glasses at them—"there aren't any family members left to corroborate Renee's story. That's either sad or convenient. Also, *our* wedding dress is clearly an early 1940s style. If Renee's grandmother married in 1955, two years after she bought her dress, then the dress was new in 1953. World War II era wedding dresses tended to have a slimmer silhouette than those from earlier and later decades."

"Fewer flounces?" Debbie asked.

"Less fabric too," Kim said. "After the war, skimping wasn't necessary. Elegant, slim silhouettes didn't necessarily disappear, but that type of wedding gown wasn't usually tea length."

"Nanny Mona's story was incredibly romantic," Debbie said. "Girl finds boy, girl loses boy because boy loses memory, boy finds memory and girl, and they live happily ever after. With all the other details, it makes you wonder if she didn't tell Renee about the pocket."

"It would have been the perfect final touch to the story," Janet said. "Are you going to wait until Renee sends the picture, just to be sure, Kim?"

"I'm going to wait, yes," Kim said, "but not for the picture. She looked at *our* picture. She studied it. She could be scouring the internet for a similar dress, even as we speak and I scarf the last piece of pizza." She held the pizza slice up like a trophy. "Renee could send us a picture from anywhere, and we'd be none the wiser."

"I don't know which title I like better for this case, if she does that," Debbie said. "The Case of the Phony Photo or the Case of the Bogus Bride."

"There's another reason to wait," Kim said. "We've been thinking that the items in the trunk have various connections. Not all to each other, but there are enough links between one and another to make us think together they have a cohesive story."

"Definitely," Janet said.

Kim wiped her fingers and sat back. "Except the wedding dress."

CHAPTER EIGHTEEN

Joyce Terrell's Diary
December 25, 1941

Today we celebrated the miracle of our Savior's birth.
Church bells woke me at midnight, and I lay in my bed
in the dark. That joyful ringing at the darkest hour of
the night kindled a spark deep inside me. I prayed that
the spark would grow. This morning I realized that
I've had my own Christmas miracle, and I know that I
will find my way forward during this dark time with
determination, strength, duty, and above all, with
joy and hope.

The Lightwoods invited me to spend Christmas
and the week before the wedding with them. I have the
loveliest bedroom, with pale blue walls and white curtains and bedspread. Theo and I opened our presents
to each other early in the morning before anyone else
crept out of bed. I gave Theo the scarf I knitted. He

immediately wrapped it around his neck. He didn't take it off all day. There wasn't enough time to knit all the warm things he'll need, wherever they send him, so I also gave him IOUs for socks and whatever else I'm allowed to send. He gave me a new edition of The Poems of Emily Dickinson *and an IOU for a honeymoon when the war is over.*

I gave Dee a pair of stockings that I'd bought in the summer and saved for a special occasion. Guess what she gave me? A pair of stockings. We laughed ourselves silly. For Mr. Lightwood, I knitted...a scarf! I gave Mrs. Lightwood an apron I made that's a twin to the apron I made for Gran. Everyone helped with Christmas dinner and cleaning up afterward.

We spent an unusual Christmas Day with so much uncertainty looming in front of us. All day our moods spun like a child's top. We'd be frantically happy, then subdued, then thankful and sentimental, and then we'd be back to frantically happy. Trying to pack as many emotions in as possible before Theo leaves for basic training and the war.

We called Gran and Grandad, and everyone took a turn saying Merry Christmas to them. Gran loved her apron. Grandad loved his scarf. He didn't notice where I dropped the stitches on December 7th. Then Gran's voice bubbled over with excitement that she couldn't hold on to any longer. She finished the wedding dress this morning! Even Grandad says it's beautiful. "When will you arrive?" she asked, knowing full well that all of us will drive down in the Green Chariot on the 2ⁿᵈ, the day before the wedding. The wedding! I can't believe our day is almost here. It wasn't a white Christmas, Mr. Burns's dear mousie, but it was joyful.

New Year's Eve
December 31, 1941

What will this new year bring? So many unknowns and one known! I shall soon be Joyce Terrell Lightwood.

New Year's Day
January 1, 1942

Theo and his father tuned in to the Rose Bowl this afternoon. Dee and I stayed to listen because she said this game was historic. It's being played in North Carolina, of all places, instead of California. For a very good reason, though! As long as the war lasts, no large public gatherings will be allowed on the West Coast, due to fears of Japanese bombing attacks. It's one more sign that nothing is normal. I feel safer here in Ohio, surrounded by farm fields and good neighbors.

Wherever Theo is sent, we can't count on him being safe at all.

We're all trying to relax after the flurry of Christmas and before the final prewedding flurry. Oh! I've just looked out the window. Flurries!

CHAPTER NINETEEN

*J*anet woke earlier than usual the next morning, thoughts of Renee and the wedding dress still stirring in her head. She slipped out of bed, padded downstairs, and fired up her laptop. Two could play the internet scouring game. She typed *WWII tea length wedding dress* into the search bar and hit enter. She opened a second window and typed *1953 tea length wedding dress*. Dozens and dozens of photographs appeared on each page. "Good luck, Renee," she said under her breath. "I hope your eyes don't glaze over as fast as mine."

"Muttering so early?" Ian asked, coming into the kitchen in slippers and bathrobe. "Is that a bad sign or good?"

"Oh dear, did I wake you? I thought I was being quiet."

"Not you, your phone." He pulled her phone from a bathrobe pocket and handed it to her.

"It's a text from Debbie. She shouldn't be up yet either." Janet opened and read the text. "This is weird. All it says is 'should we open?'"

"Come here and look outside." Ian put his arm around her and steered her to the window over the sink. "We had a little snow last night."

"A *little*?" Janet looked out at the predawn neighborhood, now transformed by a deep blanket of snow, a crescent moon shining over the scene. "It's beautiful. I want to run out and play in it."

"I'll join you," Ian said. "We can have a snowball fight."

"I'd rather make snow angels. Hang on. I'd better call Debbie."

"Hey," Debbie said when she picked up. "What do you think? Have a snow day or open and see what happens?"

"Let's! Open, I mean," Janet said. "It might be quiet, but the police and fire department won't be taking the day off—hang on, the police chief is here now. I'll ask if the department is going to work or stay home and shirk."

"The plows are clearing major roads now," Ian said. "Give them a couple more hours for the secondaries, then it will be all hands on deck. Why don't you open on a two-hour delay, and I'll give you a ride? Ask Debbie if she'd like one too."

"Did you hear that, Debbie?"

"Sure did. If you're willing to slide over to my house in the mighty Chiefmobile, I'll be ready."

"I'll wait to see that you survive the trek across the polar icecap," Ian said a few hours later when he slid to a stop outside the depot. Janet and Debbie laughed as they held on to each other and waded through over-the-knee snow. A plow had cleared the parking lot, but the walkways remained blanketed. Thinking ahead, Janet had brought a shovel so they could get the door open. They turned and waved before they went inside, first throwing snowballs at Ian's vehicle.

"We might be crazy for opening today," Debbie said, closing the door behind them.

"Nah," Janet said. "We Dennisonians always do our bit." She stamped snow from her boots and brushed it from her legs. "We can do ours by giving a free doughnut and cup of coffee to any police officer or firefighter who stops by. Snowplow drivers too."

"I love it," Debbie said.

Janet put on an apron with LIFE IS WHAT YOU BAKE IT embroidered on the bib. She ran a hand over the embroidery. "Hey, Debbie?"

"Hmm?" came Debbie's voice from the office.

"Think we'll be swamped?

"Probably not."

"Then while I get doughnuts going, why don't you compare the handwriting on the quilt blocks and recipe cards to the pocket note?"

"See if we can put a name to the note writer?" Debbie called. "Sure."

"And do it in the kitchen so I can watch while I'm baking? And start the coffee and bring me a cup?"

"Are you this bossy to everyone who wanders into the café before the winter sun comes up?"

"Sure am." Janet started humming "Wait Till the Sun Shines, Nellie" and started her prep.

Soon Debbie brought coffee for each of them and plunked down on a stool. "The beauty of having the pictures on a laptop is being able to enlarge them. That should make it easier to compare. Aww, I love these two-part notes. Didn't we decide there were two adults involved?"

"And one child learning to print. So sweet. Do they have any names on them? Are any signed?"

"No, but I'll start with these just to loosen my brains up." Debbie scrolled from note to note and back again.

Janet wanted to hang over her shoulder to stare at the screen too, but she stuck to her doughnuts.

"I'm no expert," Debbie said, scrolling back and forth slowly, "but I'm beginning to feel like one." She straightened from peering at the screen. "It's pretty obvious that the same two people wrote all of the notes, and one of those two also wrote the beginning of the note that the child finished."

"Cool," Janet said. "Should I make white chocolate raspberry scones this morning?"

"Sounds delicious." Debbie peered back at the screen. "One handwriting is casual. Dashed off. The other is more careful. It also has more loops. Do you think real experts can tell the difference between male and female penmanship?"

"They're so good, they can tell if the writer hasn't had breakfast yet." Janet put a plate of scrambled eggs and bacon next to Debbie.

"Then I'm good too, because I'm going to say the writer who dashes is male and the one who loops is female." Debbie ate a bite of eggs. "Mmm. Thank you. You should make cinnamon scones too, so people think of cinnamon toast on a wintery day."

"Perfect."

"Remember this one? The guy writes, 'Have I told you lately,' and the woman writes, 'that I love you.' I think they're a couple."

"A family, maybe," Janet said. "With a child."

Debbie nodded. "That's a theory I like. If we tell Dawn about it, I wonder if it'll jog her memory?"

"She was annoyed yesterday that we've been asking questions around town. We haven't been asking about the notes, though, so maybe this won't irk her." Janet dusted her hands. "How early do you think I can call her?"

"Not this early. It isn't even eight."

Janet looked at Debbie in mock amazement. "You nonbakers are so picky."

"Yet you still bake for us. Go figure."

Two batches of white chocolate raspberry scones and one of cinnamon later, it was closer to nine and Janet judged the hour decent enough. She called Dawn, told her their theory about the notes, and asked if she could add anything to it.

"No," Dawn said. "If you'll *remember*, I *told* you I threw *away* any notes I found."

"You did. Thanks, Dawn." Janet disconnected.

"No luck?" Debbie patted Janet's shoulder. "I'll get you another cup of coffee."

With the baking under control for the moment, Janet sat on the stool and looked at one of the two-part notes. She studied the difference between the two writers. Debbie was surely right about them being male and female. Janet scrolled through the rest of the photographs until she came to the pocket note, stopped, and scrolled quickly back to the two-part notes.

"Look who else got up early," Debbie said. "I found her at our front door."

Kim appeared behind Debbie. "Debbie says I can set up shop with my laptop at a table in the window to show people you're open."

Janet barely registered what they said. She glanced from one to the other. "I think I found it. I think I've got the connection between the wedding dress and the rest of the treasures in the trunk."

CHAPTER TWENTY

So much has happened in the space of a few days, and there's so much to say.

The wedding was a whirlwind. Quite literally! The flurries that started on New Year's Day turned into a steady snowfall, and Dennison transformed into a sparkling white wonderland. Theo and Dee and I went out walking in the moonlight after supper, kicking through the snow. We met so many people doing the same. There were pink cheeks and smiles everywhere. We went as far as Stillwater Creek, which looked like silver in the moonlight. The wind picked up on the way home— blowing straight in our faces. Theo put an arm around each of us, and Dee said we were battling our way to the South Pole to find the emperor of the emperor penguins. The wind brought more snow with it, coming down harder and faster and whipping all around us.

Later I said my prayers before climbing into bed, asking for blessings on my family and my soon-to-be family. But I couldn't sleep. My stomach had a jitter-bug going on inside, and the world outside my window had disappeared in a howl of white.

I woke up early the next morning and listened. Something was different. I heard a chair scrape down-stairs. That wasn't it. Then I knew. The difference was no sounds outside. No vehicles on the streets or turn-ing the corner. No dogs barking. No voices calling. Nothing. Out the window—we might as well have made it to the South Pole like Dee pretended. The deepest snow I've ever seen covered everything. Buried every-thing. Worse, it was still coming down. I dressed and went downstairs.

Theo and his father were in the kitchen. Mr. Lightwood listened to someone talking to him on the phone. Theo pulled me close with an arm around my shoulders. He whispered that his father was talking to someone at Village Hall to find out about the streets and roads and travel conditions. When Mr. Lightwood hung up he smiled at us. I felt Theo relax beside me, and I know he thought the same thing I did, that *everything would be fine and we'd be able to climb into the Green Chariot and drive to Steubenville.*

Mr. Lightwood said, "Well. A slight change of plans. The streets in town are hopeless. The surrounding roads too, but we'll hope they're cleared by tomorrow. Now." He waved a hand toward the stove. "Let's surprise your mother and sister by making breakfast, Theo. Joyce, why don't you call your grandparents and apprise them of the situation. With luck the snow missed them entirely."

Theo and I told him it was a fine plan.

But my call didn't go through. Not that morning. Not that afternoon. Not that evening. I didn't stop trying until it was quite late and then stopped because no one likes being wakened by a phone call in the wee hours. The snow stopped too, at some point in the afternoon. Dee noticed first.

Mrs. Lightwood added a special request when she led our blessing before supper. "For what we are about to receive, may we be truly thankful. And may the roads be cleared by tomorrow morning."

I included her request in my bedtime prayers and added another of my own. "If not clear roads, may we think up another fine plan."

In the morning, after a sleepless night for all of us, Mr. Lightwood learned that the roads out of Dennison were still blocked. He'd also heard that Steubenville had more snow than we did.

"But the wedding!" Mrs. Lightwood said. "Your grandparents, Joyce. Your dress!"

"I've just had an incandescently brilliant idea," Dee said. "We'll take the train!"

My heart leaped, but Theo shook his head. He said the train doesn't go from Dennison to Steubenville. Dee didn't want to give up. She said we could make a connection somewhere. That trains go all over Ohio. But Theo shook his head again. The train tracks were buried just like the roads, and even if, by some miracle, we made it to Steubenville, there was no guarantee we'd make it back in time for his train out tomorrow.

"If the snow is that bad," Dee said, "then there might not be a train for you to catch."

I left those two and Mrs. Lightwood in the kitchen— Theo and Dee bickering and Mrs. Lightwood telling them to keep civil tongues in their heads—and I went to try calling Gran and Grandad again. No luck, because now the Lightwoods' phone line appeared to be out. I peeked into the living room. Mr. Lightwood was there, hiding behind a newspaper he'd probably already read. I tiptoed in and over to one of the big front windows.

The children across the street had ventured out-side. The smaller ones jumped up and down on the porch. The bigger children, up to their waists in the snow, were forging a pathway from the house to the middle of the yard, where they trampled a large, round area and then waved the younger ones over. The smaller children jumped off the porch and followed the snow trench to their snowy play area. They immediately started a snowball fight.

A couple of men wallowed past, heading downtown, leaving a pathway behind them, and I got an idea. Maybe a harebrained idea, but also possibly an incandescently brilliant one. If nothing else, it would give Theo and Dee and me a reason to burn off our nervous energy and give Mr. and Mrs. Lightwood a bit of peace and quiet.

Fifteen minutes later, Theo trudged through the snow ahead of Dee and me, making a way from the porch steps to the path left by the men. From there, we turned toward town, calling Happy New Year to the few people we saw out, and heading for the Dennison Depot. From what I kept hearing, none of us had ever walked in such deep snow. It was quite an adventure.

At the depot we saw a notice stuck to the inside of the ticket window that said "All trains to and from Dennison canceled. Service to resume Sunday, January 4th."

"We're stuck here," Dee wailed. "Steubenville is only an hour away, but it might as well be on the moon." She looked like she wanted to cry.

Theo hugged me to him. I let him because it was awfully cold out, and he felt nice. But I only let him for a minute or two. Then I told them my contingency plan.

It took more effort to get to our next destination, even with Theo breaking a path ahead of us. Our breaths made feathery clouds as we went. More people were out now, with shovels and waves. When we reached Pastor Gerhard's house, we climbed the stairs and rang the bell.

Mrs. Gerhard answered the door and bundled us inside. Pastor Gerhard, looking like a hibernating bear, shuffled from the sitting room, in a pair of slippers, holding a cup of tea. We explained our problem. The Gerhards said they'd be tickled to provide the solution. Theo trudged back home to fetch his parents. Mrs. Gerhard and Dee primped my hair. Pastor Gerhard put on his shoes. Then he cut several sprigs from their Christmas poinsettia and presented them to me for my bridal bouquet.

The doorbell rang—Theo and his parents, cheeks and eyes shining. Mr. Lightwood gave me away then moved over to Theo's side to be his best man. Dee was my maid of honor. Mrs. Lightwood and Mrs. Gerhard sat on a settee crying into their hankies.

That is the story of how Theo and I got married after a howling blizzard in Pastor Gerhard's parlor. It wasn't the first wedding we'd planned. It wasn't even the second wedding we'd planned. But we'll never forget it, and you know what they say about third time's the charm.

Now, here is the reason I had so much time to write tonight. The tracks were cleared. My dear husband boarded the train at Dennison Depot this morning. Theo has gone to war.

CHAPTER TWENTY-ONE

ebbie and Kim crowded behind Janet. She opened the two pictures she'd been examining side by side. "It's all in the loops Debbie noticed in the more feminine hand in the two-part notes."

"Yes!" Kim said. "The pocket note and that one are definitely the same hand. This is exactly what I wanted to find. Stellar work, you two. If we can find a loopy quilt signature or recipe card we may just have a name."

Debbie pumped her fist. "To that I say woo-hoo, followed by it's time to open our doors."

No customers had yet come in, and Janet wondered if she'd made too many pastries. Debbie called Paulette and told her to take a snow day if she wanted to.

"Paulette's happy," Debbie reported when she disconnected. "She says she's going to be in charge of the cocoa and cinnamon toast for the three boys when they come in from sledding."

"*Three* boys?" Kim asked.

"Jaxon, Julian, and Greg." Debbie went to look out the front door. "Hey, great! Here come a firefighter and two police officers."

Debbie welcomed the trio and told them about the snow day special just for them. Janet slipped behind the counter.

"Free?" the firefighter exclaimed. "We came because we heard you were open. Didn't know anything about free. Thanks."

The trio left happy and proved to be the beginning of a steady trickle of business. Just enough to create the festive air of a snow day party, with everyone happy to have gotten out and braved the elements.

Kim stayed busy scrolling through the pictures of quilt blocks and recipe cards. During a lull, she gave a little yip. "Here's a recipe for Harvard beets from Mona Peterson and…no. The handwriting does not match any of the notes."

"One more reason the dress wouldn't be Mona's," Debbie said.

Janet refilled Kim's coffee cup. "What about Renee's story?"

"It only took me an hour to find the information I gave you last night about Mona," Kim said. "For a resourceful, creative person, it would only take a little longer to spin a tale around the basic facts."

"If she spun a story and now she's scouring the internet for a photograph, then she's putting an awful lot of effort into this." Janet sat down across from Kim. She leaned an elbow on the table and put her chin in her hand. "Not to mention gas money and mileage on her car to get here from Columbus. Doing all that to claim a dress she *might* be able to sell? For probably not a lot of money? Doesn't it make more sense that her story is true, or she thinks it is, and she's just mistaken about the dress?"

Debbie joined them. "That probably does make more sense, but spinning a tale is still a possibility. One of my former colleagues has a thirtysomething son who makes a living by reselling stuff he picks up here and there. That minimizes how much work he puts into finding the right kind of things and then advertising and shipping, but you get the idea. He started with sports memorabilia, and he's branched out since. He also tracks down specific items customers are looking for. And by makes a living, I mean he drives a new car and owns his house."

Janet took that in. "So Renee might have heard about the dress, or she might have heard about the *Days of Yesteryear* show filming here. Either way, she could have seen a trip to Dennison as a shopping trip."

"There you go," Debbie said. "If she saw something the TV experts dismissed, but she knew she had a market for, she might make an offer to the disappointed owner. She'd go home happy, and the owner would go home less *un*happy. Buy cheap, resell steep."

"Or," Kim said, "approach a museum that's just received a vintage wedding dress as a donation, spin a tearjerker story about the dress belonging to your dearly departed grandmother, adding the important detail that you're the only one who knows the story, and walk away with the dress. Tell a lie, resell high."

"Poor Renee," Janet said. "If she's really looking for her grandmother's dress, she hasn't found it."

Kim sighed. "If she's looking for it, I'm genuinely sorry. I'll email her now and be kind when I let her down."

The door opened and Harry Franklin came in with Patricia.

"Harry! Patricia!" Janet called. "I'm so glad the snow didn't keep you inside today."

"Would've been here sooner," Harry said. "Patricia helped me shovel a path for Crosby. When I say helped, I mean Patricia shoveled while Crosby and I watched from the porch. The snow's deeper than he is. We left him at home with a chew strip to make up for the weather."

Debbie brought their coffees. "Free peppermint mocha for the person who shovels so Harry can get here even on a day like this. We have doughnuts and cinnamon or white chocolate raspberry scones today."

"Ooh, cinnamon scone for me," Patricia said, taking a seat next to Harry. "Doughnut or scone for you, Pop Pop?"

"Doughnut, please. Watching people shovel is hungry business. This snow reminds me of the blizzard of '42. I shoveled Pastor Gerhard's walks and driveway, and his wife gave me an orange and a half dollar. This was back before I started working at the depot. I finished shoveling just in time too. Along came Theo Lightwood, a young man who'd just enlisted, walking with his girl, Joyce, and his sister, Dee. They walked right up the clean front walk of Pastor Gerhard's house and went inside."

"Do you think his girl's name could have been Thelma, Pop Pop?" Patricia said. "I knew an older couple named Theo and Thelma Lightwood."

Janet, Debbie, and Kim exchanged glances. Nellie's parents. What were they about to learn? All three leaned forward, waiting for Harry to go on.

"Let me think." Harry ate his first bite of doughnut with a far-away look in his eyes. "I'd heard that Theo and his girl were getting married, and Joyce is the name that sticks in my mind. My mind might be stuck, though, because several years after the war Theo moved back to Dennison with his family—two little girls and his wife. And yes, her name was Thelma."

"There could be an explanation that proves you're right on both counts, Pop Pop. Thelma might have been a second wife."

"Why haven't we heard that?" Janet asked. "Why didn't Dawn tell us?"

"Who is Dawn?" Harry asked. "And why isn't she telling you things?"

Janet looked around at the quiet café then out at the snow. "It's a good day for a story. If you two have time, would you like to hear it?"

"Nothing I like better on a snowy day than a good story," Harry said. "Put a little more coffee in my cup first, please."

Kim left her seat at the window table and joined them. Janet poured fresh coffee for everyone, and then she, Debbie, and Kim took turns telling the story of the trunk, its treasures, and the mysteries they were trying to solve. When they finished, Harry nodded.

"I like that," he said. "Nellie Lightwood was a character all her life. I didn't know her, but folks always seemed surprised by something she'd done. I'm glad to see she's still surprising people after she's gone."

"We should have asked you about her to begin with," Janet said.

"Me?" Harry sat up straighter. "I have no firsthand information. I heard stories, and I'd see her around, but there's a lot more to knowing than seeing."

"What about you, Patricia?" Debbie asked.

"I'm all in for your fashion show," Patrica said. "That sounds like fun. As for not hearing that Theo was married twice, we don't know that he was. But if he was, there might not be anything mysterious about not hearing about it. A lot of people wouldn't know, wouldn't remember, or wouldn't think to mention it. It's not like you've been putting together a Lightwood family tree. Dawn, if she knows, might assume it's common knowledge."

"It might not matter or be any of our business anyway," Janet said. "There's a fine line between being curious and being nosy."

"You've got me curious now too," Patricia said. "It should be easy enough to find out if there were two Mrs. Lightwoods. Call Dawn."

"Mm, maybe not today," Janet said. "She can be a little prickly."

Patricia laughed. "She sounds more like Nellie's niece than niece-in-law, then. I had Nellie for a class and heard her being more than a bit prickly with some of my classmates more than once. Tell you what, for a couple more scones to go, I'll take a look at court records. Let's see what I find."

CHAPTER TWENTY-TWO

*K*im came into the café shortly after it opened the next morning and slumped against the counter with a groan. "Coffee. Strong and lots of it. Please."

"Janet?" Debbie called through the kitchen door. "Have you got a minute? We have a sagging customer. She might need more than coffee to resuscitate her."

Janet came through the swinging door wiping her hands on a dishcloth. "Kim? What is it?"

"Renee replied to my email."

"Is she pushing back?" Debbie asked.

"With a bulldozer," Kim said. "A bulldozer followed by a steamroller."

"Sit down," Janet said. "Debbie's getting your coffee, and I'll be right back."

Kim sat. She put her elbows on the counter, chin in hands, and stared blankly at the yellow wall nearby. Debbie set coffee in front of her. Janet returned with a slice of French toast casserole resting in a pool of real maple syrup and slathered in butter.

"The coffee and casserole are both too hot to dig into," Janet said. "Let them sit and tell us about Renee."

"Here's the email." Kim brought out her phone, tapped into her email app, and handed it to Janet.

Debbie stood beside Janet, and they read.

Mrs. Smith,

You have no reason whatsoever to libel me by calling me a liar. My grandmother had her wedding dress made to look like one from the early 1940s. So you are wrong, and the dress currently in your collection is her dress. I cannot return to Dennison immediately, but when I do I will prove the dress is my grandmother's and therefore mine. If you do not agree, then I will be speaking to my lawyer. I hope you and your museum are well represented. I am.

"I did not call her a liar," Kim said. "In any shape or form."

"Yeesh," Debbie said. "Maybe Dawn was right about the danger of asking too many questions."

Kim took a gulp of coffee. "Too late now."

Janet handed Kim's phone back to her. "We're here for you, and it's not too late to eat your French toast while it's warm. Do that."

"Speaking of Dawn." Debbie looked toward the door. "Hi there, Dawn. You're in early today."

"That looks amazing." She pointed to Kim's plate. "I'll have what she's having."

"Coming right up," Janet said. It was nice to see Dawn in good spirits, though she still had dark circles under her eyes. Janet plated another slice of the casserole and took it and a smaller plate with butter and syrup out to her. "How are the roads between here and Yellow Springs?"

"I spent the last two nights here at the motel in Uhrichsville," Dawn said. "It made more sense than spending all that time in the car."

"Smarter with the snow too," Debbie said. "Coffee, Dawn?"

Dawn, her mouth full, raised her coffee cup in assent. "This *is* amazing," she said after swallowing. "It's the kind of breakfast that promises the day will go smoothly."

"Good," Kim said. "I'm going to hold it to that promise. See you later."

"Keep us posted," Janet called to her back.

"Will do." Kim waved over her shoulder and left.

Janet bussed Kim's dishes and wiped the counter. "How's the work going at the house?"

"Getting there," Dawn said. "But there's always one more room, one more cupboard, one more overlooked space to clear out."

"Would you like me to come help this afternoon?" Janet asked.

Dawn put her fork down. "After the way I groused at you over the phone yesterday?"

Janet nodded.

"Count me in too," Debbie said.

"Then I can't think of a good reason to say no."

"Do we ask her about Joyce?" Debbie asked as they drove to the Lightwood house that afternoon.

"Let's wait until we hear from Patricia. Dawn was almost cheerful this morning. Let's give her a break from our questions while we're giving her a hand."

Dawn opened the front door and waved them in as if she'd been watching for them. "I'm working in the main floor library today. Ready to tackle more books?"

"You bet," Janet said. "But a favor first? Can we see the attic?"

"There's always a catch to free labor." Dawn sighed. "Kidding. You're giving me your time. Letting you see the creepy attic seems fair. Put your coats in the kitchen and come on up."

They found Dawn waiting at a door midway down the upstairs hallway. "What are you looking for up there?" Dawn asked.

"Not looking for anything in particular," Janet said. "But I'd like to see the little door. The one where you found the trunk."

"Don't be disappointed," Dawn said. "It isn't anything more than that. Here we go. More stairs to climb." She opened the door, flipped on a light, and started up.

Janet gasped. "The risers!"

"The what?" Dawn asked.

"Risers," Debbie said. "The uprights that face us that the stair treads sit on."

"If you say so."

Each of the risers in the staircase to the attic had been decorated. The first half dozen looked like bookshelves, with the spines of books painted on them. "I can read the titles. There's *The Miracle Worker*," Janet said.

"There are scenes from Dennison farther up," Debbie said, climbing past Janet. "Here's the depot, this one's the Christmas train. Harry and Crosby sitting on their bench!" Debbie took a picture of the riser with her phone. "This is wonderful."

The public library appeared on one riser, on another the old high school where Nellie had taught, and painted on the riser above that was a school auditorium with the cast of a play on stage holding hands at the end of a production. The last riser showed an attic with a jumble of old furniture and, in one corner, a tiny door.

Janet looked from that last painting into the attic and back to the painting. "It's this attic. It's the little door where you found the trunk. Did Nellie paint these?"

"Every last one of them." Dawn shook her head. "Typical Nellie."

"What do you mean?" Janet asked.

"She didn't think ahead," Dawn said. "Can you imagine the effort it's going to take to sand down or paint over all that? Sand and paint both probably. Typical Nellie."

"I was just thinking how much I'd like to get my risers painted like this," Debbie said.

"Probably regret it," Dawn said.

Except for a set of metal utility shelves and a box tipped on its side, the attic was empty. Huge too, as Ian had said. The ceiling—the underside of the roof—rose steeply from waist-high around the outside walls to ten or twelve feet in the center. Janet crossed to one of the four gable-end windows and looked out on the neighborhood. Children in the backyard next door worked on a snow fort.

Dawn, hands on her hips, glanced around the space. "I should've taken a before picture up here. You wouldn't believe the amount of stuff the family carted up here over the decades. The place was packed. Based on the age of most of the items, the bulk of it was Nellie's garage sale rejects."

"Did you know that Nellie volunteered for the high school theater program?" Debbie asked. "She found the props they needed and clothes for costumes."

"Yes, but that doesn't explain the broken and bizarre stuff that followed her home." Dawn gave the box a kick. Empty. She picked it up. "Who brings home a cracked flowerpot or a toy dump truck missing a wheel? Or boxes and bags of snarled balls of yarn?"

"She actually did something wonderful with the discards and rejects she brought home," Janet said. "She finished unfinished projects and mended things. Brightened things up with paint."

"Then what did she do with them?" Dawn asked.

"She gave them away, anonymously, to surprise people who needed a bit of joy," Janet said.

"There was a secret knitter in town some years back," Debbie added. "Someone who left handknitted hats and mittens for people to find. We think that was Nellie too."

"First I've heard of it." Dawn looked at the empty box in her hand. "And it doesn't change the fact that she ended up with more stuff than she could have fixed or prettied up in two lifetimes."

"And left it for you to deal with," Janet said. "And that's a lot."

"May we look inside the little door?" Debbie asked.

"Crawl all the way in if you want," Dawn said. "The spiders won't care. There's no light."

Using their phones as flashlights, Janet and Debbie crouched through the door.

"It really is a crawl space," Debbie said, "but not a claustrophobic one. Think we'll find another note? One that got lost in a back corner?"

They looked at each other, dropped to their knees, and crawled all the way to the end.

"Nothing left but dust," Janet said.

Debbie sneezed then giggled. "And barely enough room to turn around. Let's get out of here. It's freezing."

"An odd place to keep a trunk," Dawn said when they reappeared. "You keep asking questions about it so here's what I think. Stowing the trunk all the way at the back of that dark tunnel wasn't so much about keeping it out of sight as putting it out of mind." She looked at their pant legs. "Brush yourselves off, and let's get busy."

Janet stopped on the attic stairs to take pictures of a few more risers then rushed after Dawn and Debbie.

"More books." Dawn dropped the empty box she'd brought down from the attic. "Most of these were Nellie and Barbara's parents' and grandparents'. Same drill as last time. Check for anything Nellie tucked inside, but otherwise box them up and move on to the next shelf."

Janet went to the shelf on the left side of the fireplace. "Are you sure? I see leather spines."

"If they're worth something, they're not worth my time to find out."

"Well," Janet said. "They'll be a nice donation to the library book sale."

"After going through this cleaning out process, you can bet I'm streamlining my own stuff back home," Dawn said. "I'm streamlining my will too. It'll be right there in black and white—who gets what, where to donate things, and what to toss."

"No option for a garage sale?" Debbie asked.

"Up to my heirs. If they want the hassle of a garage sale, more power to them. I won't be around to stop them."

"Nellie didn't have details like that in her will?" Janet asked.

"I'll be generous and say she might have planned to but put it off until too late."

"What about inviting Nellie's former students to come in and help themselves to the books?" Debbie asked. "I read a mystery, set in the Highlands of Scotland, where someone did that. She had what she called a decanting and decluttering and invited her friends to help themselves to whatever she didn't want anymore."

"I suppose in the Highlands they can get away with the decanting part," Dawn said. "The whole thing sounds incredibly iffy. People wandering around and taking things. Who's to say those friends wouldn't tell other friends and before you know it you don't know who's in your house. Like the teenage parties you hear about that get out of hand."

"You could be right," Debbie said. "The book was a murder mystery and, sure enough, someone died during the decanting and decluttering."

Janet found the rhythm of clearing shelves again—remove an armful of books from a shelf, flip through them, pack them away, go back for another armful. She found a few bookmarks, a business card for an insurance agent, and a crisp, new-looking 1944 dollar bill. "Here's a dollar for you, Dawn. Freshly printed in 1944."

Dawn didn't look up from flipping pages in her own stack of books. "Give it to Kim at the museum."

"Really?"

"You should know the answer to that by now. One dollar? I can afford to be generous with that, and a 1944 dollar bill probably fits Kim's collection policy perfectly."

The next book in Janet's stack was as tall and wide as a legal pad, but thicker. The faux leather cover was black with red faux leather corners and spine. "Cool. I found an old ledger."

"Flip through it and put it in the box," Dawn said. "If I stopped to gape at every oddity I tripped over I'd still be clearing the attic."

Janet flipped, but slowly. Precise notations for merchandise sold, prices, and dates filled the pages of columns and lines—entries for fabric, spools of thread, coffee beans, bags of flour, sugar, canned peaches, a pair of suspenders. She flipped back to the beginning but didn't find the name or location of the store. The first entry, for a pound of butter, was dated July 28, 1951. Too late to be of interest to Kim even if the store had been local. She came across several blank pages in the middle of the ledger, and then a second person began making entries. "Whoa."

"What?" Debbie asked.

"Hang on." Janet flipped pages. The second set of entries had columns for items bought, brief descriptions, prices paid, addresses, one of four sets of initials—YS, ES, RS, or O, and date. The first date was July 27, 2002. "Dawn, is this Nellie's handwriting?"

Janet took the ledger to Dawn. Debbie came to look too.

Dawn glanced at one of the pages. "That's Nellie. What is this?" She took the ledger, looked at the cover, and flipped through the first few pages.

"Nellie used the second half," Janet said.

"Another one of her UFOs." Dawn shook her head and handed the ledger back.

"Her what?" Debbie asked.

"Unfinished objects. That's what she called the junk she couldn't pass up that everyone else ran from. Unfinished? More like unhinged."

"May I have it?" Janet asked.

"Why?"

"The last time we were here you said we could take books home if we wanted them."

"I mean, out of all the books here, why that?"

"Curiosity more than anything," Janet said. "It looks like a record of the yard sales and estate sales Nellie went to. In fact, I bet that's what the initials are for. YS for yard sale, ES for estate sale. What would RS and O be for?"

"Hmm. Rummage sale and other?" Debbie said.

"Yes!" Janet said.

"If that ledger is what gives you a thrill," Dawn said, "it's yours."

"Did Nellie have a desk?" Janet asked. "A ledger seems more like something to keep in a desk than on a shelf in here."

"I found a birdhouse in the linen closet," Dawn said. "So a ledger on a bookshelf seems downright normal. She did have a desk though. One of those old rolltops with drawers and pigeonholes. It's the one piece I almost kept."

"Why didn't you?" Janet asked.

"It was a monster. No room. I found Barbara's letters to Nellie in the pigeonholes. Do you think they could have helped solve your little mysteries?"

Dawn, still flipping pages, missed the stricken look on Debbie's face at the words "little mysteries." Janet saw the look, and gave Debbie's arm a squeeze.

Going back to her bookshelf, but mindful she shouldn't take too much time, Janet opened the ledger again. She flipped through the pages of Nellie's entries, scanning each quickly. And there—there! She was tempted to shout *yahoo* but didn't. She marked the page with the dollar bill and went back to work.

Sometime later, Dawn stretched and put a hand to the small of her back. "Enough for today. Ladies, you haven't caught me at my best since I've been here. But I appreciate you."

"Our pleasure," Janet said. "You're going back to Yellow Springs tomorrow?"

"And I'll be back here Monday morning."

"Drop by the café for a lunch break when you return," Debbie said.

They retrieved their coats and purses then said their goodbyes. Janet raced toward the car, ledger in hand. She threw open the passenger side door and got in.

Debbie opened the driver's door a moment later, her cheeks red as she laughed. "Why the hurry? Couldn't get out of there fast enough?"

Janet felt like she'd been biting her tongue since she'd marked the page in the ledger with the dollar bill. She turned to her friend and let it spill. "I have the address of the house where Nellie bought the quilt squares and the recipe box!"

"Whoa!" Debbie exclaimed. "Should we drive by and see if we want to ring the doorbell?"

"Wild horses couldn't keep me away," Janet said. "Giddyap."

CHAPTER TWENTY-THREE

We're looking for 4-1-1," Janet said as Debbie turned onto a side street. "It should be in the next block on the left." Debbie slowed and Janet sat forward, checking addresses. "There, the white one. Cute porch. The lights are on, and someone just pulled the curtains. Do we stop?"

"Might as well," Debbie said. "There's a free space right in front, and we're itching for answers. I'll turn around in the neighbor's drive."

After pulling into the space, Debbie glanced at Janet, who nodded. They got out of the car and walked up the shoveled front walk and onto the porch. Janet hesitated only a moment before ringing the doorbell.

A young woman with a toddler girl attached to her leg swung open the windowless inner door. She looked from Janet to Debbie and blew her bangs off her face. The bangs fell back where they'd been. The toddler, eyes big, stuck her thumb in her mouth. The woman opened the glass storm door just wide enough to speak through. "You're not the grocery delivery."

"Sorry, no," Janet said. "Although we are in the food business."

The woman's face broke into a smile. "The café! I knew I recognized you. Um, what can I do for you?"

"We have an odd question about something bought at a yard sale here ten years ago," Debbie said.

"The mother of all yard sales?"

"Sorry?" Janet said.

"That's what we called it. If you don't mind talking in the kitchen, come on in." She backed away from the door, taking the toddler with her.

Janet and Debbie followed them to a blue and white kitchen smelling deliciously of sautéed garlic and onions. "We're Janet Shaw and Debbie Albright, by the way," Janet said.

"I'm Christy, and this little pumpkin is Lulu. We're making spaghetti sauce, aren't we, Lu?" Lulu hid behind Christy's legs and peeked at Janet and Debbie. "We had a yard sale when we bought the house to get rid of the stuff the previous owners left behind. Kind of a massive undertaking and not exactly successful. My husband dubbed it the mother of all yard sales."

"What a bother," Debbie said.

"Right? Especially in August. Hot, muggy, and buggy." Christy stirred the sauce and blew at her bangs again.

"August?" Janet said. "Not June?"

"No, it was August. We closed on the house at the end of July."

"Do you remember selling several dozen quilt squares with embroidered names on them and an old, painted recipe box with recipes in it?" Janet asked.

"We can show you pictures," Debbie said. "If that will help."

Christy shook her head. "I wish they'd left behind something that cool for us to find. They left us broken appliances large and small, a bathtub, car parts, motor oil, hubcaps, half-empty paint cans. We thought we'd try to sell it before paying someone to haul it away. We added some of our own stuff to make the sale more attractive. But no quilt squares or recipe boxes."

"Do you have an address for the previous owners?" Debbie asked.

"It was two brothers. The house had been their mother's. She passed a few months before they put it on the market."

"Do you happen to know what their mother's name was?" Janet asked.

Christy's eye searched the corners of the room and came up with the answer. "Norton. Stella Norton. The sons had a different last name. You'd think I'd remember their name more than hers."

"Do they live in the area?" Debbie asked.

Christy shook her head. "They flew in from wherever, did the bare minimum to get the house ready, then vamoosed. Their lack of interest worked in our favor, though. The price came down quite a bit because they couldn't be bothered."

"Couldn't be bothered with their own mother's house, and they sold her box full of recipes." Debbie shook her head.

"They weren't very sentimental," Christy said, "and so many people don't have the time or space for sentiment these days."

"That sounds like a kind way to put it," Janet said. "Are you from Dennison originally?"

"Steubenville, but I love it here. You couldn't drag us out of this town with ten elephants, could you, Lulu?" Christy said, swinging Lulu up into her arms and giving her a kiss on her plump cheek.

Lulu gave her mother's cheek a loud, juicy kiss and grinned.

"We're glad to have you here too," Debbie said. "Welcome to Dennison, ten years late."

Christy's bubbling spaghetti sauce had smelled so good, Janet scrapped her original plans for supper that night and put her own sauce on to simmer. While it gently bubbled and sent its tantalizing, tomatoey aroma swirling through the room, Janet scanned the rest of Nellie's ledger entries for the wedding dress.

"No luck," she said to Ranger. The cat twined around her ankles. "Thank you for your sympathy, but do you know what?" Ranger sat and blinked at her. "I'm not disappointed. I didn't want to find out that Nellie bought the dress at a rummage or yard or estate sale. I want the wedding dress to be more special than that. To have a better story behind it."

She was humming to herself, and just taking garlic bread from the oven, when Ian came in the back door.

"Mamma mia," he said, sniffing the air and closing his eyes. "I don't know what I did to deserve you."

"You made it home for supper. That's good enough for me. I've missed you. I've been having fun with Debbie and Kim too, but there's been a big, Ian-shaped hole in my evenings lately."

"Sorry, love. There's another budget meeting next Wednesday evening."

Simultaneously, Janet and Ian said, "Budgets," and sighed, then looked at each other and laughed.

As Ian finished a second helping of spaghetti and mopped the last of the sauce from his plate with the bread, Janet asked if he'd ever known the Norton family. "Her name was Stella. She passed ten or eleven years ago."

"Stella Norton." Ian thought for a moment. "The name rings a bell, but I can't think why. Who was she?"

Janet told him about helping Dawn that afternoon, finding the ledger, and about Nellie's notes in it. "Remember the things we found in the trunk from Nellie house? She noted quilt squares and a recipe box in the ledger, bought at an estate sale at Stella's house after she passed. We spoke to the woman who lives in the house now. She and her husband bought it from Stella's sons ten years ago, in July. The estate sale was in June. So we think Stella's sons had their sale before they sold the house."

"Solid detective work," Ian said.

"It feels like we're getting closer to finding out about the wedding dress. Oh! Ian, when you checked Nellie's house after the intruder, did you see the paintings going up the attic stairs?"

"I don't remember any paintings in the house at all. But then I was more concerned with finding a person. One who wore an elusive scent."

"Nellie painted the risers of the attic stairs." Janet showed him the pictures she'd taken. "I wish I'd taken pictures of all of them. Debbie took a picture of the painting with Harry and Crosby in it."

Ian handed her phone back. "They're charming. I'm sorry I bounded past them on my way up." His eyes twinkled. "Are you getting ideas about our stairs?"

"Debbie is about hers. I wonder if the painting on the top riser is a clue."

"How so? A clue leading where?"

"Leading to the trunk," Janet said. "It's the only one of the paintings that shows the house in any way, and it shows the little door to the crawl space in the attic. It's not like she painted the door in eye-killing, neon pink to draw attention to it or anything. But she does draw attention to it by having it in the picture."

"If she wanted to be sure someone found the trunk, it might have been wiser to tell someone about it," Ian said.

"True. So maybe just a fun visual clue. But maybe she did tell someone about the trunk, and not just where to find it, but the significance of the things in it."

"That's a possibility," Ian said.

"And we just haven't found that person yet." Janet thought of Nellie's stroke and her frustration when she couldn't make Dawn understand what she was trying to say. Maybe Nellie hadn't told someone but had tried to.

Janet looked up from adjusting a tray of scones in the bakery case when Kim walked into the Whistle Stop Café Saturday morning. "You're radiating calm and confidence this morning, Kim."

"Makes a change from yesterday, doesn't it?"

"Coffee?" Debbie asked.

"Please." Kim sat at the counter. "Do you want to know my secret?"

"We love secrets," Janet said. She remembered their visit to Bonnie at Sticks & Threads. Bonnie had started to say she'd found fabric that almost matched the old apron from the trunk. She'd stopped, annoyed with herself because Kim had asked her to keep it a secret. Were they about to be surprised?

"The secret to my calm and confidence is that I'm not going to worry about Renee anymore. I'll wait for her next move. If there even is one. She might have been blowing hot air in her email." Kim squinted at Janet. "You look disappointed, Janet."

"Me? No." Janet gave herself a little shake. "Not at all."

"What if she isn't blowing hot air?" Debbie asked.

Kim took a sip of her coffee and smiled. "That's the second part of my secret. That's what documentation and lawyers are for."

"Dare we hope she doesn't come back?" Debbie asked.

"Hope is good," Kim said. She toasted them with her cup and stood.

"But you can't go yet," Debbie said. "We have news too. Risers first, Janet?"

"Yes."

"Show her the pictures, then, and I'll go get the monetary donation for the museum."

"Monetary donation?" Kim asked.

Janet chuckled. "Yes, ma'am. Now look at this. Nellie painted the risers on the stairs to her attic." She handed over her phone.

Kim scrolled from picture to picture. "Oh. My. Goodness."

"Dawn's only thought is how hard it'll be for someone to get rid of the paintings."

"Why would anyone get rid of them?" Kim asked. "Who cares what their attic steps look like, anyway? These are fantastic."

"Dawn's under a lot of pressure."

Debbie came back with the dollar bill and the ledger. "Look what Janet found in a book over there yesterday. Dawn doesn't want it." She handed the 1944 dollar bill to Kim.

"Still crisp," Kim said. "How cool is that? Thanks."

"One more surprise." Debbie handed the ledger to Janet. "You found it. You should show her."

Janet showed Kim the book then opened it to Nellie's entries. "Where, when, and what she bought at yard, rummage, and estate sales." Then, while Debbie got coffee for a customer, Janet related their adventure of the day before, ending with the visit to Christy and Lulu.

"This is great," Kim said. "I'm thinking it raises more questions than it answers, though."

"Is your first one whether I found the wedding dress in the ledger?" Janet asked.

"Wait," Debbie said after rejoining them. "Did you?"

"No."

"Good," Debbie said.

"Exactly what I told the cat last night," Janet said.

"Why?" Kim looked from one to the other. "Wouldn't knowing *something* about the dress be better than nothing?"

"We want to know a more interesting something," Debbie said.

"More special," Janet said. "With a real connection to Nellie. Somehow."

"Okay. I can't argue with that," Kim said. "More questions, then. If Nellie bought the quilt blocks and recipe box at a garage sale, why did she put them in the trunk? Why that particular collection of things? Are we any closer to knowing that?"

"It feels like we are," Janet said.

"And you can trust her feelings because she's married to the chief of police," Debbie said.

Kim laughed. "I can't argue with that either. One more question. Who is Stella Norton? Are we assuming the recipe box was hers? And how did she end up with the quilt blocks? And don't tell me that's three questions. I counted them myself."

"Here's a fourth," Debbie said. "What do we do when we're looking for information like that?"

Janet raised her hand. "I know! I know! We access Dennison's own database. We call Eileen."

CHAPTER TWENTY-FOUR

Joyce Terrell's Diary
April 8, 1942

A change of scenery. I have come back home to Gran and Grandad. Why? Because there's a great big change in store for me, for all of us. Or little, depending on how you look at it, because babies are such perfect but very tiny creatures. I'm going to be a mama! I'm helping Gran and Grandad with the boardinghouse, and Gran with her sewing business, and slowly changing shape. I don't mind admitting that the changes, although gradual, are a bit alarming.

I haven't been writing as often these days and weeks. I've been saving my thoughts for letters to Theo. He is over the moon about the baby. I write to him every week, and live for his letters back, and pray every night for his return.

May 1, 1942

The government starts rationing sugar this month. Gran says it's a good thing we're all sweet enough as we are. Beyond that news, this is our life of late:

> *Collecting War Savings stamps issued by the US Treasury to help fund the war.*
>
> *Pasting the stamps in a booklet so we can eventually redeem them for War Bonds.*
>
> *Cooking for the boarders, cleaning, laundry, sewing and more sewing.*
>
> *Listening to the war news on the radio.*
>
> *Laughing with Grandad at Jack Benny in the Jell-O Program on the radio.*

In closing, we have ants in the kitchen. Proverbs reminds us that we should observe the ant and be wise. I am happy to do that. Just, please, not in the kitchen.

May 19, 1942

Had a funny letter arrive from Dee today, full of beauty tips she read in a magazine. If you run out of lipstick, use beet juice to stain your lips. If you haven't run out of lipstick, use it on your cheeks as well as your lips for added color. Out of liquid stockings or need a tan? Use brown gravy as a self-tanner. When I read the tips to Gran, she said the magazine should have added four words to that last tip—stay away from dogs.

June 9, 1942

Amazing news! Dee joined the Women's Army Auxiliary Corps. She ships out for training in Des Moines, Iowa, in July. She can train to be a clerk, a typist, or a driver. Nursing is out because she's never taken nursing classes. She says that's peachy with her. She's already an excellent typist, and if that's what the WAACs need her to do she'll do it happily. What she really wants, though, is to be a driver. She'll learn to drive Jeeps! Jeepers!

August 13, 1942

I feel as plump and red as one of the ripe tomatoes in our victory garden.

September 3, 1942

A letter arrived from Theo today to make my birthday extra special. Dee and Mama Lightwood sent cards. I feel as if I've aged a decade in the last year.

CHAPTER TWENTY-FIVE

*E*ileen says she's been wondering how we're coming with our mysteries." Janet slipped her phone into her pocket. "She'll be waiting for us this afternoon. She also said she'll round up the usual suspects. I was about to ask what she meant, but she laughed and hung up."

"She gets a kick out of sleuthing." Debbie glanced out the window. "Good! Here come Harry and Patricia. I can't wait to show Harry the picture of him and Crosby."

Janet had coffee waiting for Harry and Patricia by the time they sat down at the counter. "Debbie has something special to show you, Harry."

"And I've got information for you." Patricia took a notebook from her purse and set it next to her peppermint mocha.

"Well, now," Harry said, cradling Debbie's phone. "There's a couple of handsome fellas, if I do say so myself."

"Let me see, Pop Pop." Patricia took the phone. "Is that a painting? Where?"

Debbie told them about the stairway paintings. "I'll send the picture to you, Patricia."

"That Nellie," Harry said, "still surprising folks. Should I worry that I spend too much time sitting on that old bench?"

"No," the three women said.

Harry added his deep laugh to theirs. "Wasn't going to stop anyway."

Patricia picked up her notebook. "Ready for my report on the Theodore Lightwood family?" At their nods, she read from her notes. "Theodore James Lightwood and Joyce Macbeath Terrell were married in Dennison on January 3, 1942."

"The day of the big blizzard I told you about," Harry said. "That was something else. The kind of snow that sticks in your mind for eighty-plus years. The trains couldn't run for two days, and I made a lot of money shoveling for folks."

"This is the sad part," Patricia said. "Joyce died in childbirth on August 16, 1946."

"Tragic," Janet said. "Did the baby survive?"

"Was that baby Nellie?" Debbie asked.

"To answer your questions in order, yes and no," Patricia said. "Nellie Macbeath Lightwood was born October 4, 1942. Her sister Barbara was born in 1946. In 1948 Theo married Thelma June Hanson."

Harry put his arm around Patricia. "She does good work, doesn't she?"

"I do *great* work, Pop Pop, if I say so myself. I also found real estate transactions. In June 1948, Theodore Lightwood bought a house on North Second Street in Dennison."

"That's not many blocks from our house or his parents' house," Janet said.

"But where did he and Joyce live?" Debbie asked.

"Steubenville, Ohio." Patricia flipped her note over. "I found two earlier real estate transactions. The first, in December 1945, has

Theodore Lightwood buying a house in Steubenville. The second, in May 1948, he sells that house."

"So after the tragic death of Nellie and Barbara's mother, he remarried and returned to Dennison," Janet said.

The new information certainly offered additional context to the fabric of Nellie's story. But it still wasn't clear how all the pieces fit together.

The usual suspects at Good Shepherd that afternoon turned out to be Ray and Rita in addition to Eileen. Janet felt so happy to see Rita looking cheerful, she gave her a big hug. Then, to be fair, Janet hugged Eileen and Ray too.

"Rita," Eileen said, "may I introduce you to Debbie Albright? You already know Janet. The two of them own the Whistle Stop Café down at the depot. Debbie, I'd like you to meet one of our newest residents, Rita Chaffee."

"So nice to meet you, Rita," Debbie said.

"Likewise," Rita said.

"Clary would have joined us too," Eileen said, "but she's teaching backgammon to some of the residents. Show them what you're working on, Rita."

A smile spread across Rita's face as she smoothed her hand over the pieced fabrics held in the small quilting frame on her lap. "A baby quilt for my newest great-grandchild on the way. What do you think of the hot pink and bright green? Plenty of zing?"

"Enough zing to make it sing," Debbie said. "How do you like it here at Good Shepherd?"

"It couldn't be better," Rita said. "Moving is never easy, but I'm glad to be back in Dennison, close to family and among friends old and new. Janet, what do you think of the quilt?"

"I love it," Janet said. She wondered if the bright colors were the influence of the library quilters. Seeing Rita so animated gave Janet an idea about the quilt squares. She made a mental note to discuss it with Debbie and Kim.

Ray had his eye on the white bag Debbie had in her hand. Debbie noticed and held the bag up. "Janet made roasted pear scones this morning. Any takers?"

Everyone was a taker. Ray finished his first.

"What's the name you're after?" he asked. "Norton? I remember Stella Norton. She was Stella Close before that."

Janet took notes.

"And before that, she had an Italian last name," Rita said.

Debbie looked at the list Kim had made of the quilt signatures and recipe card names. "Could it have been Estrella Bernardi?"

"That's it," Rita said.

"Of course." Eileen nodded. "She always preferred Stella to Estrella. She was a sweet thing."

"A sweet thing who meant well," Rita agreed. "She was also... unusual."

"How do you mean?" Janet asked.

"These days she might be diagnosed with something," Eileen said.

"Kleptomania," said Ray.

"Most likely," Eileen agreed. "But often, people made allowances for her."

"Possibly not either of her husbands," Ray said. "I think they both took advantage of her. Her parents left her well-off. The husbands left her less well-off."

"That's terrible," Debbie said.

"We'd been wondering who had and took care of the quilt squares all those years," Janet said. "We think, now, that it was Stella."

"That sounds like Stella," Rita said. "Good-hearted."

"She might have taken good care of them," Ray said. "But taking them might be how she happened to have them."

After the service at Faith Community Church Sunday morning, Janet stopped by the teen knitting group. Bonnie at Sticks & Threads had looked at the scarf Janet found and suggested the yarn might be some she'd sold the adult leader. Janet watched the teens knitting and chatting with each other. She was no expert, but these young people appeared to be excellent knitters. The teacher smiled when she noticed Janet and came to the door.

"I just have a quick question," Janet said. "I don't want to take you away from them."

"They'll be fine. Let's step out in the hall. You're Janet Shaw, aren't you? I'm Mindy Vale. I don't think we've met."

"Nice to meet you, Mindy. It's kind of an odd question, and if you know the answer but don't want to tell me, that's perfectly okay."

"This is intriguing."

"The whole thing is intriguing. Do you know anything about the anonymous mittens and hats that have been appearing around town?"

"Ah, the mystery knitter. I don't, but don't you love it?"

"I do, and I'll be happy leaving it a mystery, but I'm trying to solve another puzzle that involves one of my old high school English teachers—Nellie Lightwood. Did you know her?"

"I'm sorry, no."

"Well, thanks, Mindy. It was worth a try. Did you teach the kids to knit like that?"

"Except for the ones who already knew, yes. Even the guys are into it." She laughed. "They call themselves the knitting dudes."

Janet glanced over at the young people. She recognized one, though she didn't have a name to attach to the face. "Who is that girl in the center? Looks like she's helping another girl with her project."

Mindy looked around the edge of the door. "Oh, that's Piper. She's my star and right-hand knitting tutor."

"Do you think I could talk to her? Just for a minute."

"I don't see why not." Mindy caught Piper's attention and waved her over. "This is Mrs. Shaw," Mindy said. "And this is Piper."

"It's so nice to meet you, Piper. I'm hearing great things about your knitting."

"Thanks."

Piper was the girl who'd missed her coffee refill when Renee first showed up at the café.

The girl who'd skittered away from her at the theater rehearsal.

And the girl at the basketball game Jaxon had bought the popcorn for—unless there was another Piper Jaxon knew. She hadn't gotten a good look at her at the game. She decided to gamble. "I think you know friends of mine—Jaxon and Julian Connor?"

"Oh. Yeah."

Mindy touched Janet's arm. "I'm needed inside. Dudes dueling with needles."

"Thanks, Mindy." Janet expected Piper to slip back inside too, but she didn't. "That's a nice scent you're wearing, Piper."

"My mom gave it to me for Christmas. It's called Garden Sunlight."

"The name captures it perfectly. It smells exactly like a delicate whiff of sunlit flowers. I'm Janet Shaw. We met Wednesday at the Whistle Stop Café."

"You bake really good cookies."

"Thank you. I'm sorry you didn't get the refill on your coffee. I also got the feeling that you wanted to speak to me."

"Um. Kind of."

Janet saw Piper's uneasy glance at her fellow knitters. Some of them were openly watching their exchange. "Tell you what," Janet said. "I know you like coffee."

"Almost as much as homemade cookies."

"Then if you don't have plans this afternoon, would you like to join me for a cup of coffee at the new shop near the library? We'll see if they have homemade cookies, and you can ask me your question then."

"That would be nice."

"How does two o'clock sound?"

"I should check with my parents, but I'm sure it's okay."

"You check with them and send me a text." Janet gave Piper her number. "Hope to see you there. I might have a question for you too. About knitting."

With her smile, a dimple appeared in Piper's right cheek.

Piper's text confirming their two o'clock meet-up arrived as Janet and Ian finished lunch. Janet hadn't seen Debbie at church, but called her to ask if she'd like to come along.

"Sorry, plans with Greg. But sample their wares and let me know what they're like. Why are you meeting with a high school girl?"

"On a hunch."

"I like hunches," Debbie said.

"Me too. Also, because she wants to talk to me. I'll fill you in."

A few hours later, Janet showed up at the new coffee shop, fifteen minutes before the appointment, and nursed a coffee and cookie for nearly an hour.

Piper never came.

CHAPTER TWENTY-SIX

While alone in the kitchen Wednesday doing the morning's baking, Janet mulled the question of Piper's no-show at the coffee shop. Maybe she'd had second thoughts about meeting. Or a more interesting opportunity had come up. Perhaps she'd even gotten sick. There was no way of knowing. Piper hadn't sent an explanation or apology. The young woman seemed like a shy animal that needed coaxing. Janet measured out walnuts for the brownies and the morning's scones then decided to toast them for extra oomph.

"Morning, partner," Debbie sang as she came in the door. "Have I ever told you how good this kitchen smells every single morning?"

"Every single morning, silly. And that's the aroma of toasting nuts you smell today."

They were so busy, the morning flew by. Kim came in at lunchtime, looking slightly less calm and confident than she had on Saturday. She took a seat at the counter. "Soup and a sandwich," she said when Debbie asked what she'd like. "And I know this is the worst time, but when you or Janet find a minute, can we go over the menu for the fashion show one more time?"

"Absolutely."

Not long after, Janet plunked onto the stool next to Kim. "Shall I save you some anxiety? Ingredients have all arrived. Anything I can prepare ahead is prepared. Barring unforeseen circumstances, everything else will be ready on time."

"Ready and delicious," Debbie said in passing.

"I knew they would be," Kim said. "Thank you. It's the unforeseen circumstances giving me the yips. One of the models backed out this morning. For some reason an emergency appendectomy is more important."

"Good to see your sense of humor isn't suffering from the yips," Janet said. "That's important."

"What can I get you now, Kim?" Paulette asked as she cleared away Kim's empty dishes. "In my book, hard work calls for a little something extra. How about one of Janet's maple walnut scones? Made with toasted walnuts."

"If you also prescribe a little something extra for the nerves, like some of that maple compound butter, then yes."

Paulette returned with the treat. "The fashion show is going to be a hit. It's too bad that there aren't any men's or boys' clothes in that trunk. I would have loved roping Greg and my grandsons into the show."

"And I would love to know your roping technique," Janet said.

"Don't you worry," Paulette said. "I will teach you my wily ways."

Janet patted Kim's arm. "Be back in a few." She took her turn ringing up orders, checked the bakery case, and started more coffee brewing.

"How are ticket sales?" Debbie asked.

"As of this morning," Kim said, "we're sold out."

"That's great!" Janet and Debbie high-fived each other.

"It makes me nervous."

"Kim, why?" Janet asked. "You've done lots of programs."

"This one has more moving parts than most, and there's still the threat of Renee out there waiting to pounce."

"Email her," Janet said. "Ask her to meet you one day next week, after the show, to discuss ownership of the dress."

"I did. She sent a two-word reply. 'As if.'"

"If she wants the dress, why is she being so antagonistic?" Debbie asked.

"That's what I can't figure out," Kim said.

"Change of topic then," Janet said. "You don't need that negative energy. If the museum isn't going to accession the quilt squares, why don't we ask Rita Chaffee and the quilters who meet at the library to finish the quilt? Then we can auction it with the proceeds going to the high school theater department."

"In honor of Nellie?" Debbie asked.

Janet nodded. "What do you think, Kim?"

"I think that kind of positive energy will see me safely through the fashion show."

Beaming, Janet carried empty bakery trays to the kitchen. Too excited by the quilt idea, she took a moment to call Clary Spencer and Dorothy Simms, the two women who, like Rita, had each made one of the quilt squares. Clary loved the idea but had to rush off for the Good Shepherd book group. Dorothy, with more time on her hands, chatted a bit.

"It's so good to know what became of the quilt squares," Dorothy said. "Stella had them all those years. My goodness."

"Just as you stitched a piece of the quilt, you gave us a piece of the puzzle we were trying to solve," Janet said.

"And, thanks to you, our blocks will finally form a finished quilt. What about the recipe cards? I imagine it will be much harder to find out whose they were."

"We think they were Stella's," Janet said. "Nellie bought the recipe box at the garage sale her sons had after Stella's passing."

"Well, I continue to learn something new every day."

"What do you mean?" Janet asked.

"Did you know Stella?"

"No."

"Well, years ago, way back, you could not get that woman into a kitchen," Dorothy said. "I wouldn't call it a phobia, exactly. Eccentricity, maybe. So I'm glad to learn that she got over it and took up cooking."

As the lunch rush wound down, Janet noticed Kim now sitting at a table in the window with her laptop. "I didn't realize she was still here," Janet said quietly to Debbie. "What's up with her?"

"Getting a bit of work done while continuing to draw on our positive energy," Debbie said. "I did wonder if she was hiding out here in case Renee showed up at her office. But the café isn't exactly a dark hideaway."

"Especially a window seat."

The door opened and so did Janet's mouth. She immediately closed it then smiled and waved to Courtney McCampbell, the theater teacher, and Piper.

"Hi!" Courtney said with a bounce in her step and in her voice. "Piper and I are here on sort of a field trip."

"Wonderful," Janet said, wondering what the theater teacher and the young knitting whiz had in mind. "What can I get you?"

"Coffee, Piper, or hot chocolate?" Courtney asked.

"Hot chocolate, please." Piper's eyes strayed to the bakery case.

"Two hot chocolates," Courtney said, "and two of whatever looks good to Piper in the bakery case, please."

"I just brought out fresh cookies," Janet said.

"She makes the best cookies," Piper said.

"Then I need to taste them," Courtney said. "We also each have something to tell you. Can you join us briefly? Both of you? It's a lot to ask when you're busy, I know. It's about Nellie's trunk of clothes."

"You go, Janet," Debbie said. "I'll join when I can."

"Both of you go," Paulette said. "It's quiet enough, and I'll cover."

"Can we make it a table of five?" Janet asked. "Kim Smith, the director of the museum, is right over there. Nellie's niece-in-law donated the trunk to the museum."

"That's great," Courtney said. "She should definitely hear this."

"Kim? We're invading," Debbie said.

Janet made the introductions, and Kim closed her laptop and set it aside. Debbie brought a fifth chair over and sat next to Janet.

Courtney took a sip of her hot chocolate then put both hands on the table. "When I heard about the fashion show, and then heard that the clothes in the show are from the trunk that you told me about—" One of Courtney's hands went to her chest. "I mean, 1940s-era clothes that are worthy of being in a fashion show? Including a wedding dress that people are saying might be valuable?" Courtney shook her head. "I want you to know that I know there's no way Nellie would ever have bought clothes like that for high school theater costumes. When we talked at the rehearsal, I'm pretty sure I made it sound like the clothes should belong to the theater department. I'm sorry about that."

"Hey, no worries," Debbie said.

"Debbie's right," Kim said. "I've been hearing about the terrific job Nellie did for the theater department. Thinking the clothes were meant for the school was an easy and logical mistake to make."

"Phew. I'm glad to get that off my chest." Courtney smiled and nudged Piper. "Piper has something to tell you too."

Piper hesitated, her eyes darting from one to the other.

Janet stepped in. "I was sorry not to see you at the new coffee shop on Sunday, Piper."

"That's what I wanted to tell you. I'm sorry I didn't make it."

"I was worried that something might have happened to you," Janet said gently.

Piper looked uncomfortable and wrinkled her nose. "I was worried when my dad told me you're the police chief's wife. And at the basketball game, Jaxon said his dad was there with the chief and they were walking around asking people questions about Nellie."

"Why did that worry you?" Janet leaned closer to Piper. "You should know that he's more like the chief of teddy bears than the chief of police."

A quick smile came and went from Piper's face. "I was worried because I've been to Nellie's house."

Janet sensed Piper's hesitation to say more. Rather than jump right to the question of why Piper was worried, she softened her approach. "It's an amazing house, isn't it? Debbie and I have been helping Nellie's niece-in-law, Dawn, clean it out. But why were you worried about being there?" The scent Piper's mother had given her for Christmas tickled Janet's nose, bringing a flash of insight—had that been the scent Dawn smelled when she discovered the footprints? "Have you been to Nellie's house recently?"

Piper bit her lip. "Yeah. I missed Nellie and missed the Workshop of Unfinished Dreams in the attic. That's what Nellie called it. And I saw a car there."

"Dawn's been putting in long hours at the house," Janet said.

"Before she died, Nellie said she knew *someone* would have to do *something* with all the stuff she was going to leave behind," Piper said, becoming more animated as she relaxed. "She said she didn't envy them doing that, and she figured it would be Dawn because Dawn is a helper and a good soul."

"It would mean a lot to Dawn to hear that," Janet said.

"I was going to tell her and thought maybe she'd let me look around," Piper said. "She didn't answer when I knocked on the back door. Nellie never kept it locked, and Dawn hadn't locked it either, so I opened it and went in. I was about to call out hello and introduce myself but I heard Dawn on the phone. I don't know who she was talking to, but she sounded pretty angry so I snuck back out."

"Oh, Piper. What were you thinking?" Courtney asked. "Did she hear you come in? Was she calling the police?"

"That's just it. I don't think she heard me at all, and it didn't sound like she was talking to the police. She wasn't answering questions or giving the kind of information you would to the police. She was angry at the person on the other end and yelling. Nellie had said Dawn was a good soul, but she didn't sound like it and I didn't want her to yell at me."

"I don't blame you," Debbie said. "What can you tell us about Nellie?"

"She talked a lot."

The others laughed.

"When she taught at the high school and was the prop manager, she went to yard sales and flea markets and places like that to find props and costumes for the plays. Then she retired, and her sister died. Nellie said she felt lost for a while but pulled herself together. She started volunteering for the high school theater department and going to yard sales again. That's when she got her idea to look for UFOs—Unfinished Objects. She said being eccentric is a perk of being old. She loved finding projects that people hadn't finished— knitting, embroidery, models. Broken things too. She finished the projects and fixed the broken things then gave them away."

"Anonymously," Janet said.

Piper nodded. "She kept it a secret. She liked surprising people by bringing them joy."

"But she told you," Janet said. "You must feel honored."

Piper nodded again.

"If she kept it a secret, why did you come tell us?" Kim asked.

Piper hesitated, looking less sure of herself again, then turned to Janet. "You've been trying to find out about Nellie, and I decided that I didn't want to be the only one who knew what she was really like."

"So you came to surprise us and bring us joy," Janet said.

"Nellie said shine your light because you never know who the glow and warmth will be cast upon."

"That's beautiful," Debbie said. "Thank you, Piper."

"Did she tell you about the trunk in the attic?" Kim asked.

"Only that she had it and called it her *own* unfinished object. Well, that isn't exactly all. She gave me something from the trunk before she had her stroke. She said she found it in the trunk with a note from her father. It's her mother's diary. She said that every diary is essentially unfinished so it's a UFO too. It's my favorite color of blue and has 'Five Year Diary' stamped on the cover in gold leaf." Piper's smile shone. "Did you know Nellie liked quotations?"

"I would have thought *loved* was the right word, there," Debbie said.

"Debbie and I had Nellie for English in high school," Janet explained.

"You're so lucky!"

"One of my favorites that she told us is from Helen Keller," Janet said. "'Keep your face to the sunshine and you cannot see a shadow.'"

"Mine is the second part of Luke 12:48," Piper said. "'From everyone who has been given much, much will be demanded; and from the one who has been entrusted with much, much more will be asked.' Nellie said that means when you're blessed then it's your responsibility to bless the next person."

Janet thought about the anonymous mittens and hats being left around town. "Piper, there was a question I wanted to ask you. May I ask it now?"

"Sure."

Janet checked the tables around them then leaned closer and asked quietly, "Are you the anonymous mitten and hat knitter who is surprising people with joy?"

The dimple showed in Piper's cheek. She whispered back, "Can you keep a secret?" The four women solemnly nodded. "I'm carrying on Nellie's tradition."

Courtney squeezed Piper's shoulder. "Don't forget you brought something for them too."

Piper pulled her backpack onto her lap, unzipped it, and brought out a bright blue book. "When Nellie gave it to me, she told me it's my turn to write in it. I thought you'd like to read it."

"Her mother's diary?" Janet asked.

"Now Piper's diary," Debbie said. "You don't mind if we read what you've written in it?"

"I haven't written anything in it yet. Nellie's mother started writing in it on her birthday. Nellie started her entries on *her* birthday. I'm waiting. My birthday is January thirty-first."

"We'll take very good care of it and get it back to you before then," Janet said. "Thank you, Piper."

Kim had been looking at Piper and Courtney in a sizing-up kind of way. "You've both heard about the fashion show we're having Saturday afternoon, right? If I had two more volunteers, that would bring me terrific joy."

CHAPTER TWENTY-SEVEN

"Budget meetings are the bane of Ian's existence," Janet told Debbie when she invited her for supper. "But what a boon for us. Come over and we can spend the evening reading the diary aloud to each other."

Janet served up plates of Welsh rabbit—a creamy, cheesy sauce spooned over her homemade English muffins.

Debbie served up compliments. "This cheese sauce not only grabbed my nose and dragged me in the door when I arrived," she said, "it is divine, and the English muffin base is to die for."

"It is pretty spectacular, isn't it? But if we start serving this at the café, let's not use the phrase 'to die for.'"

"To live for, then," Debbie said.

"*That* I like. I can see an apron with 'I Live for Cheese' on it in my future. Make yourself comfortable in the living room. I'll be right in with cocoa."

"On my way," Debbie said, then called, "Perfect! Ranger's already here waiting for a lap."

Janet brought a tray with mugs of cocoa and a plate of brownies. They shed their shoes and settled at either end of the sofa, the cocoa and treats in easy reach on the coffee table.

"Do you ever think we should stop sampling so many of our wares?" Debbie patted her stomach.

"We don't sample that many, you haven't gained an ounce, and we need to be familiar with what we offer so we can make informed recommendations when our customers need help making up their minds."

"You are very wise," Debbie said. "I agree with every point. What does your wisdom tell you about the angry phone call Piper heard? What was Dawn so angry about that it scared that girl right out of the house?"

"It could have been anything. Dawn said it herself on Friday. She hasn't been at her best. Kim described her as brittle. Ian said prickly. We've both seen all of that and more."

"And Piper is skittish," Debbie said. "So whose part of the diary should we read first, Nellie's or her mother's?"

"Nellie would tell us not to cheat by skipping ahead. Start at the beginning and let the story build. You know, it's just occurred to me that we don't know which mother this is." Janet hadn't opened the diary yet. She hadn't wanted to ruin the surprise of meeting Nellie's mother for the first time. "This could be Thelma."

"Only one way to find out," Debbie said.

Janet opened the bright blue cover, and a smile spread across her face. "Not only one way to find out, Debbie. Two. This *is* Joyce's diary, and I'd recognize her handwriting anywhere. Take a look." She passed the diary to Debbie.

"Fantastic!" Debbie said. "Our mysterious pocket note author. One mystery solved and it's a very satisfying answer. No, wait. You know what this means, right? This is proof that it's Joyce's wedding dress. Should we call Kim?"

"I think you're right, but let's read first. There could be another explanation for the note to be in Joyce's handwriting."

"Like what?" Debbie asked.

"I can't think of anything that makes as much sense as the dress belonging to Joyce. But her grandmother was a seamstress. What if the dress was for someone else, or a sample that was never worn, or—"

"I still think it's Joyce's dress." Debbie handed the diary back to Janet.

"I do too. Let's read and see if we find out for sure." Then, while Debbie sipped her cocoa and her own grew cold, Janet read Joyce Terrell's diary aloud. They heard the happiness in her words as she talked about her job, her friends, and the boardinghouse where she lived. The budding romance between Joyce and Theo tickled them, but also made Janet's heart ache.

"Flurries!" Debbie said when Janet read the entry for New Year's Day, 1942. "Is that Harry's blizzard?"

"Has to be."

"Then keep reading."

Janet turned the page and read the entry for January 5, 1942 and Joyce's description of her joyful wedding despite the great blizzard. At the end of the entry Janet looked up. "Those last lines are a good example of the amazingly positive attitude people had during the war. 'It wasn't even the second wedding we'd planned. But we'll never forget it, and you know what they say about third time's the charm.'"

"How cool that Harry was there to see Joyce and Theo walk to the minister's house," Debbie said. "And then Theo left for the war."

"At least we know that he came home, but they had so little time together after that. Do you want me to keep reading?" Janet asked.

"Yes, but after a short break. I need to give Greg a quick call."

When Debbie returned, Janet asked if she wanted to read. Debbie shook her head. "This is like story time. If you don't mind reading."

"I don't mind. Here we go."

Janet smiled when Joyce wrote that she was expecting and moved back home to Steubenville with her grandparents. She and Debbie commiserated over the start of sugar rationing, laughed at Dee's beauty tips involving beet juice and gravy, and celebrated with Joyce on her twenty-first birthday.

"How are we for time?" Janet asked.

"Ranger and I are fine." Debbie stroked the cat purring in her lap. "But let's give your voice a break, and I'll read over your shoulder."

"Okey doke."

September 10, 1942

Nellie MacBeath Lightwood arrived in this world at dawn on September 4th.

Gran says she is absolutely perfect. Grandad says she has the lungs of an opera singer. And what do I say? That I did not know what love was until I held her in my arms and looked into her eyes. She makes me want to sing, so I sing lullabies to her. Sometimes "Wait Till the Sun Shines, Nellie," and sometimes our own version of it that starts with "Wait Till Your

Papa Meets You." Nellie is unimpressed with those words and falls asleep.

For such a small human being she takes up an awful lot of time, space, and energy. While she naps (and when I'm not napping too), I've been making aprons for Gran's sewing business. They're my own design. I feel very clever having produced a perfect baby and an apron pattern that's selling like hotcakes. Gran and I have been sewing pretty clothes from flour sacks too. Gran is kind and tells me that someday I'll fit back into my own pretty clothes.

I also did a special, secret sewing job with a scrap of white Gran had left over. It's something for Nellie to discover when she's older. When it's time. And from now on I'll keep this diary for Nellie and address my entries to her.

"The pocket in the wedding dress!" Debbie said, pointing to the letter. "It has to be, and she says the note was for Nellie. That's the proof, don't you think? The dress belonged to Joyce."

"I agree. Do you think Nellie found the note?"

"Yes," Debbie said. "I do. Let's keep reading."

October 15, 1942
Dear Nellie,
We had a letter from your aunt Dee today. She's being kept on in Des Moines as a driving instructor. Can you beat that? She has big plans for her twenty-fifth birthday. A quarter of a century! She's having the time of her life but

doesn't mind telling me that she misses home. Misses family.
Misses me and aches to meet you. But she's throwing herself
a birthday party, and I know that will cheer her right up.

    Your loving Mama

Janet waited for Debbie to let her know she finished and then turned the page. "I wonder why this page is outlined in black."

Debbie, eyes going wide, asked, "What's happened?"

Janet swallowed and read the next part out loud.

"'November 18, 1942. Dearest Nellie, I can't bear it. Dee is gone. Killed in a road accident in Des Moines.'"

"No." Debbie said. "How sad."

Janet wiped a tear and smoothed the page. "Joyce didn't even sign that entry." She turned the page. "There's a huge gap after that. Almost two years. She doesn't write again until June 6, 1944."

"D-Day," Debbie said.

"You okay?" Janet asked.

"Yeah. But I wanted to ride in the Green Chariot with Dee."

Janet blew her nose. "I know. Ready?"

Debbie nodded, and together they looked at the letter.

    June 6, 1944
    Dear Nellie,
    These are some of the words from President Roosevelt's
prayer today: "And let our hearts be stout, to wait out the long
travail, to bear sorrows that may come, to impart our cour-
age unto our sons wheresoever they may be."

Wherever your papa may be, Nellie, I know he loves us and prays to come home to be with us every single night. Maybe every single minute of every day. The same way we pray that he comes home safe and sound, but mostly that he comes home one way or the other. And Gran and Grandad and Aunt Dee up in heaven pray for that too.

Your loving Mama

"Gran and Grandad?" Debbie said when they reached the end of the letter.

"No wonder she didn't write for so long." Janet grabbed a handful of tissues. "Thank goodness we didn't try to read this between customers at the café. Can we take any more?"

"We can't stop now."

"'May 8, 1945. Dear Nellie, The war in Europe is over. Praise God. Your loving Mama.'"

"I'm glad we know that Theo came home," Debbie said. "Waiting and wondering is so hard."

"Whether you're reading a diary or experiencing it in real life," Janet agreed, knowing that Debbie was remembering the pain of waiting and wondering and then losing her fiancé, Reed, to the war in Afghanistan so many years ago. "The next entry is in August."

August 14, 1945
Dear Nellie,
The whole war, the whole terrible, horrible war is over! Japan has surrendered unconditionally, just as Germany did

in May. My darling, your papa will be coming home! It can't
happen right away, but it can't happen soon enough either.

    Your loving and grateful Mama

"What an amazing undertaking it must have been to bring everyone back home again," Janet said.

"And not just home to the US," Debbie said. "Troops were going home to Canada, Great Britain, Australia. It was a massive, world-wide migration. Does it say when Theo got back?"

"In November. That's the next entry."

    November 9, 1945
    Dear Nellie,
    Did you see the love in your papa's eyes when he met you?
More love than there is water in all the oceans. We are a fam-
ily, home at last. Whole at last.
    Your loving Mama

"Debbie!" Janet exclaimed. "Joyce and Theo both write the next entry."

    December 25, 1945
    Dear Nellie,
    You are the most
    perfect Christmas present imaginable.
    Your loving Mama
    and Papa

"Joyce wrote the first part, up to 'most,' and 'Your loving Mama,'" Debbie said. "Theo wrote, 'perfect Christmas present imaginable' and 'and Papa.' It's a prototype of the two-part notes to come, don't you think?"

"I don't know if it's the first time they did it, but Theo's handwriting here matches the two-part notes, and they started writing them *some*time. If it started here, I think Theo interrupted Joyce when she started this entry."

"Turn the page and see if they keep it up," Debbie said.

"Hold on. We've forgotten about the other note with the wedding dress. The one that fluttered out the first time we held it up. We never compared that handwriting."

Debbie was busy with her phone. "Here it is. 'But still my fancy wanders free through that which might have been. Thomas Love Peacock.'" Debbie looked at the diary and back at the picture of the note on her phone. "It's Theo. No doubt about it."

"No wonder it's so melancholy. A love lost. He did gain another, but still, a love lost. Let's keep reading."

> *January 1, 1946*
> *Dear Nellie,*
> *So much news for the new year! We've sold this drafty old barn of a boardinghouse and we're going to move into our very own snug little house. And you're going to be a big sister!*
> *Your loving Mama*

"Not written in tandem," Debbie said. "But a diary written like that would be a little odd."

March 11, 1946

Dear Nellie,

This evening I sat knitting for the baby and watched as your papa read to you. How many four-year-olds do you suppose take a shine to the advice of Arnold Bennett? I borrowed the book after we put you to bed so I could get this quotation exactly right. "A first-rate organizer is never in a hurry. He is never late. He always keeps up his sleeve a margin for the unexpected." How you giggled over that! I have no idea why, but I also have no doubt that Papa will use that advice in his new job managing the S.S. Kresge store downtown.

You bring so many unexpected pleasures to our lives, Nellie. I love seeing your papa reflected in you.

Your loving Mama

"No wonder Nellie loved that quotation," Janet said when she saw Debbie finished the letter too. "She learned it at her papa's knee as a four-year-old. I'm not sure I knew anything loftier at age four than 'Twinkle, Twinkle Little Star.' Now we skip forward to May."

May 6, 1946

Dear Nellie,

I hope you remember this advice if you need it in twenty or so years. Planting a garden with a three-year-old calls for keeping an enormously large margin for the unexpected up your sleeve. It also calls for a bath for everyone involved. After that adventure, Papa left this note on the edge of the bathroom sink, *"Our child is"* and I added, *"muddy and marvelous."*

Goodnight, darling.

Your loving Mama

"I can see getting into writing notes like that," Debbie said. "I wonder what Greg would think of it?"

"Try it and see."

Debbie turned the page. "What? Wait." She turned the next. "Blank?"

"She'd been writing less and less frequently," Janet said. "Busy with a four-year-old, busy getting to know her husband again, the new house, the garden. Throw in a dash of morning sickness and the fun of writing notes back and forth."

Debbie flipped another page.

"Debbie." Janet put her hand on the diary so Debbie couldn't turn any more. "That's all there is."

CHAPTER TWENTY-EIGHT

The next morning, Debbie came through the back door of the café without her usual cheery greeting, and earlier than Janet expected. The oven timer went off. Janet took two pans of muffins out and slipped two more in. "Morning, partner. The coffee's ready."

"Great. Would you like some?"

"Please."

Debbie returned with two steaming cups.

"I brought the diary." Janet looked at the clock. "There might just be time to read it between batches of muffins and scones. I've got them on trays all ready to go in the oven, and I can get to the cookies later."

"Is it safe? The diary took us on a bit of a roller coaster ride last night."

"It did, but I have insider knowledge. I cheated and turned the page. Just one. I think we can take a chance on Nellie's section having a happier ending."

"It won't really have an ending," Debbie said. "Remember what Nellie told Piper? Diaries are all, essentially, unfinished. That makes some sense. Even if someone is scribbling away right up to the end, something still happens when they drop the pen."

"I see your point, but that's beginning to sound a little morbid."

"Is this better?" Debbie asked. "Maybe Piper will leave pages empty for the next person to fill, and it'll become the never-ending diary."

"Much better."

They sat side by side with the diary open on the table in front of them.

Janet turned the page and saw a watercolor painting of a sunlit kitchen and a young woman, standing with her back not quite turned to the artist, stirring something at the stove. The soft colors made the small painting look like a memory, distant but not in any way distorted.

"It's exquisite." Janet turned the page to another painted image. In this one, an elderly woman working at a sewing machine had just looked up with a smile for the artist. On the next page an elderly man, behind the wheel of a pickup truck that looked equally old, smiled and waved out the window.

"Wait. Turn back to the first picture," Debbie said. "Look at the apron."

Janet peered at the young woman's apron made of yellow, red, gray, and white plaid fabric with bright red binding. "It's *the* apron. Is that Nellie at the stove, or—" Janet turned pages to look at the woman sewing and the man in the truck. "These are Joyce's gran and grandad, don't you think?"

"Then it must be Joyce wearing the apron," Debbie said.

The next page showed a young couple standing on the doorstep of a small bungalow, each with a hand on the shoulder of the little girl in dungarees standing in front of them.

"The house they bought in Steubenville," Debbie said.

"Look at Nellie's face. The mischief is plain to see."

Janet turned the page and felt a little stab of sorrow as she gazed at a watercolor of five gravestones in the dappled light of an oak tree, one with the name *Joyce Terrell Lightwood*.

"Joyce. Aw," Debbie said. "The other names are Terrell too. They must be her parents and grandparents. Turn the page. Find something happier."

With every page they turned, they saw another part of Nellie's life in her beautiful washes of color. Next was a picture of a man with a baby on his shoulder.

"Theo and baby Barbara," Janet said.

The next two pages showed a little girl and a toddler sitting in a red wagon, then a young woman sitting on a porch swing with the same children.

"Thelma," Debbie said. "I'm glad Nellie and Barbara look so happy."

The next pages showed exteriors of the Lightwood house in Dennison, the front porch of the house in summertime with hanging ferns, rocking chairs, a little table with a vase of colorful zinnias, and then an older couple reading in tall wingback chairs in the library, their faces lit by a cozy fire in the fireplace.

"Theo and Thelma?" Janet asked. "Old so soon?"

"I think it's Theo's parents," Debbie said. "Remember Theo bought a house here. Dawn did say the books we packed on Friday were mostly Nellie and Barbara's parents', so maybe Theo and Thelma moved there after his parents passed. We didn't read much about his parents in Joyce's entries after she moved back home with Gran and Grandad."

"People were so busy with the war effort. Joyce probably didn't get back to see them. They probably didn't go see her either. People had to save their tires from wear and tear because they were hard, if not impossible, to get."

"I'm sure their hearts shattered when Dee died." Debbie turned the page to find a younger couple, again, and two little girls at a beach. The woman in the picture wasn't very much taller than the girls were.

"Here's our answer," Janet said. "This is Theo and Thelma. The girls are stretching as they grow. Dawn said Thelma was short, and she's not much taller than Nellie, now."

"I doubt Dawn knows about this diary. Nellie gave it to Piper before she died and before Dawn found the trunk. Don't you think it was a little strange that Nellie gave a family diary to a kid who isn't related?"

"It is," Janet said. "Dawn says they weren't close, though. Maybe she didn't disguise how she felt about Nellie's collecting habits, or about collecting anything herself. If Nellie thought the diary would just be tossed, she might have seen Piper as someone who would appreciate it. A kindred spirit."

The next pictures showed a young Nellie at the front of a classroom, then a wedding with Nellie beside Barbara, the bride.

"Not the dress in the trunk," Debbie said.

The next dozen pages were of birds, flowers, and a succession of cats napping, yawning, stretching, and washing. The cat pictures were neatly labeled, in black ink, with the cat's name. The first picture of each cat also included a birth or adoption date. The last picture of each cat gave the date of its passing.

"Cats, cats, cats," Debbie said. "No dogs?"

Janet laughed and flipped the page. "The trunk!" The painting showed two views of the trunk, closed and then open.

"Quick, turn the page," Debbie said. Janet did, and Debbie crowed, "Yes!"

The following pages showed everything they'd found in the trunk and each picture was labeled in the same neat printing. The clothes were arrayed across two pages. The label at the bottom read *Joyce Terrell Lightwood's clothes. Many sewn by her or her gran.* The recipe box and the apron appeared together on one page. That label read *Thelma Lightwood's recipe box and Joyce Lightwood's apron. Two mothers, who showed their love every day, always together in my heart.*

"She loved them both," Janet said. "I'm so glad."

"But the recipe box! If it's Thelma's, how did Stella Norton end up with it?"

"I guess our mysteries aren't over yet," Janet said.

The quilt blocks appeared in an arc surrounding one larger block—the one with Thelma's embroidered name. The label read, *Another UFO has landed!* An asterisk at the bottom of the page was followed by *UnFinished Object. What happened? A mystery I didn't have time to solve. I leave it in your hands.*

"Is she talking to Piper?" Debbie asked. "For goodness' sake, Nellie, why didn't you date your pictures?"

"That's a mystery *we* might never solve," Janet said with a laugh.

The next page showed the two-part notes labeled, *Theo and Joyce's private game.* The diary itself appeared after that, bright and blue, with no label at all. Then came a picture of an older man closing the lid of the trunk and a picture of the door to the attic crawl space. Neither picture was labeled.

"The wedding dress isn't here," Debbie said. "She must not have known it was in the trunk. She never found that sweet note in the pocket. I don't like that at all."

"That makes the note another unfinished project," Janet said. "If Nellie is up there looking down, I bet she thinks that's a pretty good joke on her."

The last three paintings were of Piper.

"The rest of the pages are blank for Piper's entries," Janet said. "What a lovely gift Nellie gave her."

"Why didn't she date all the pictures the way she gave dates for the cats?" Debbie asked. "The trunk pictures, especially. She could have painted them years before she painted Piper. But if she found the trunk soon after Thelma died, that might explain why she started calling her Thelma instead of Mama."

"Go back again, though," Janet said. "To the last picture of the last cat."

Debbie flipped back. "Rejoyce. I just got that—Joyce, Rejoyce."

"There's no date for her passing," Janet said. "Go back to the first picture of Rejoyce."

"Nellie adopted Rejoyce in 2020," Debbie said, "and the trunk pictures come later, so she found the trunk sometime after that. Good detective work, Mrs. Chief of Police."

"But did you hear what I said? There is no date for the cat's passing. Debbie, where is Rejoyce now?"

CHAPTER TWENTY-NINE

Piper might know where Rejoyce is," Debbie said. "She probably does or she would have asked about her yesterday, don't you think? Maybe she even *has* Rejoyce."

"Then she would have *told* us yesterday," Janet said. "Adopting a friend's cat is a pretty big thing." She looked more closely at Debbie, who quickly looked away. "Speaking of pretty big things, you think I'm making too much out of this."

"No, no." Debbie put her hand on Janet's shoulder. "I think we're both emotional after reading the diary. Some of Kim's pre-fashion-show jitters might be in play too."

"I'm not jittery over the show. The food is well in hand. I'm not worried about Renee either. Kim has *that* situation well in hand. I'm not emotional about a cat I haven't met. I'm worried about its welfare. Besides, if someone has her, then we might have another person who can tell us about Nellie."

"So call Piper," Debbie said.

"It's a school day." Janet turned to the trays of scones ready for the oven. "I'll finish today's baking."

"Sounds good. I'll get things ready out front."

Janet waited for the swinging door to close behind Debbie then said to the scones going into the oven, "And while you lot are baking, I'll call Dawn." She took out her phone and pressed Dawn's number.

"Good morning, Janet," Dawn said. "Seems like we're getting to be old friends."

"Although, when you think about it, we actually are."

"So we are. Who knew we'd ever run into each other again? I'm back in Dennison for the next few days."

"The final push?"

"Dream on," Dawn said. "I bought a ticket for that fashion show. Thought it might be fun to see the clothes strutting down the catwalk."

"Kim does a great job with her programs. I'm sure this one won't disappoint." Janet suddenly realized that Dawn might hear about Joyce for the first time at the fashion show. How would that go? She decided to break the news now.

"Still there?" Dawn asked. "What's up?"

"Something interesting. Debbie and I read Joyce and Nellie's diary."

"Nellie kept a diary? Who's Joyce?"

"Joyce was Nellie and Barbara's birth mother. She died when Barbara was born." To the silence on Dawn's end of the call, Janet related a brief version of Joyce's story based on the records Patricia had found. "The clothes in the trunk belonged to Joyce."

"Then I guess...." Dawn's voice faded out.

"It's a lot to take in," Janet said.

"Where did you get the diary?" Dawn asked.

"Nellie gave it to a friend who lent it to us."

"And where did you find this *friend*?"

"The friend found us," Janet said. "After hearing that we were interested in Nellie."

"Heard about your questions, you mean. Are you sure this friend didn't hear the questions, put two and two together, and decide that an unoccupied house would be easy pickings? Found that diary when they broke in that day?"

"We saw the footprints, Dawn. That person didn't go any farther into the house than the middle of the kitchen."

"That could have been a second visit and they took off when they realized I was there."

Rather than argue, Janet changed the subject. "Dawn, what I really called about is Nellie's cat, Rejoyce. Do you know where she is?"

"The *cat*? You spring this diary on me then ask about the *cat*? The neighbor across the street took it. She spends the winter in Florida. The cat went with her."

"Thank you, Dawn. Sorry to bother you."

Janet pocketed her phone as Debbie came through the swinging door. "The neighbor across the street has Rejoyce," Janet said. "They're spending the winter in Florida. Wouldn't you love to see a watercolor of Rejoyce lounging under an umbrella at the beach?"

"I would dearly love to see that."

Janet pointed toward the diary. "Kim should read it too. I'll run it over to her and be right back."

In between customers, Janet told Debbie about Dawn's reaction to hearing about Joyce and the diary. "If Dawn was even half as angry when Piper heard her talking on the phone, it's no wonder the poor girl crept out of the house."

"It makes me think Piper and Dawn need to meet under optimum conditions," Debbie said. "Piper needs to see that Dawn isn't all bark, and Dawn needs to hear from Piper what Nellie said about her."

"Dawn's here at least through Saturday night. She's coming to the fashion show."

"Interesting," Debbie said. "I wouldn't have pegged her as the fashion show type."

"Then again," said Janet, "are any of us?"

The rest of the morning flew by without much time for conversation. After the lunch rush, Debbie leaned against the counter and took a sip of coffee. "I've been thinking."

"And what are those thoughts?" Janet asked.

"That my coffee is cold."

"Deep thoughts." Janet bussed the dishes from the counter and wiped it.

"Also that Kim probably needs a distraction before the show, and we'd like Dawn and Piper to meet. So I asked myself how we could take care of both issues in one efficient get-together."

Friday evening, Janet helped Debbie carry dishes of chicken stroganoff, roasted broccoli, and warm sourdough bread from Debbie's kitchen to the dining room. Janet filled the water glasses, and Debbie called her guests to the table. Kim, Dawn, Courtney, and Piper took seats on either side. Debbie sat at the head and Janet at the foot.

Debbie smiled at each of them. "Thank you all for accepting my invitation. Let's say a blessing, then please help yourselves and pass the dishes along. For what we are about to receive, and for friends new and old, may we be truly thankful."

Dawn helped herself to the stroganoff. "This looks and smells wonderful. Thanks for including me." She handed the dish to Kim and took the broccoli from Janet. "What's the occasion?"

"Tomorrow is the fashion show," Debbie said, "and we are all, one way or another, involved or responsible for it happening."

"I guess I know what part I played," Dawn said. "I'm the only one who knew anything about the trunk. And I know how you three are involved." She waved a hand at Debbie, Janet, and Kim then gestured to Courtney and Piper. "What about these two?"

"Courtney has agreed to be the emcee," Kim said, "and Piper is one of our models."

"Emcee?" Debbie said. "I thought you'd tapped them both for models."

"Courtney's theater background makes her perfect for the emcee," Kim said. "And that leaves me free to keep everything else moving. I've just had an idea, though. Awfully last minute. Janet and Debbie let me read the diary this afternoon, Piper. I brought it to give back to you, but maybe Courtney would like to borrow it to glean background for her remarks during the show."

"That would be fantastic!" Piper said. "It's a short read, Ms. McCampbell."

"It might be just the touch I need to give the show extra sparkle," Courtney said. "But Dawn, there's more to our involvement with Nellie. Piper is in my theater program at Claymont High School, and Nellie volunteered for the program."

Dawn nodded. "I heard about her volunteer work. Surprised me."

Courtney's eyebrows raised.

"Surprised me in a good way," Dawn rushed to say.

"Nellie was one of those volunteers you dream of," Courtney said. "Efficient, perceptive, creative, capable of self-direction in the *right* direction so that she eased the load instead of making more work. She wanted to make it to one hundred. I wish I could have wrapped her in a quilt, or bubble wrap, to make that happen."

Dawn passed the bread across the table to Piper. "What did you young folks think of Nellie?"

"We thought she was awesome," Piper said, more to the bread than Dawn. "Whenever Nellie came to the school we knew we'd have a good day." Then Piper looked up, took a deep breath and said to Dawn, "I came into Nellie's house one day when you were there. She and I were friends, and she told me something I thought I should tell you."

Janet saw Dawn go very still. "You came into the house?"

"You were on the phone and you sounded angry, so I decided not to bother you and left."

"Oh, honey, I sound angry more often than I should. If you need proof of that, ask Janet what happens almost anytime she calls me. So I wonder what bee I had in my bonnet that day?" Dawn squinted into a corner of the ceiling then clucked her tongue. "I was talking to my daughter. She'd just told me, too late of course, that she wished I'd kept the letters Nellie's sister Barbara wrote to her. How on earth was I supposed to guess *that* when she's never shown any interest in writing letters herself? Live and learn. Did I scare you?"

With a look at Janet, Piper said, "A little."

"I'm sorry. So what did you want to tell me?" Dawn asked.

"Nellie told me that she knew someone would have to clean out the house when she passed, and she didn't envy them that. She figured it would be you because you're a helper. She said you're a good soul."

Dawn started to speak and stopped. Finally a soft, "Thank you," came out.

"Can I tell you something else?" Piper asked.

Dawn had trouble speaking again, and Piper didn't wait. "I knew about the trunk. Nellie told me—"

"Oh my goodness," Janet blurted. "Sorry to interrupt, Piper, but Nellie tried to tell Dawn something after her stroke. She couldn't get the words right and it frustrated both of them." She turned to Dawn. "Nellie didn't say *pilot* and *junk*. She'd told Piper about the trunk. She tried to say *Piper* and *trunk*."

"That's better than anything I've come up with," Dawn said.

"We still have the mystery of the recipe box," Kim said. "Janet and Debbie, you caught that discrepancy when you read the diary, didn't you? If the box was Thelma's, how did Stella Norton end up with it?"

Piper raised her hand. "I know. Nellie told me. She was so happy when she found the quilt squares and the recipe box at the garage sale. So glad she got them before anyone else snapped them up. She didn't know anything about the squares except one of them had her mother Thelma's name embroidered on it. She remembered the recipe box, though. It was Thelma's, with recipes Thelma collected. Nellie hadn't seen it since she was a girl and took it to a Girl Scout meeting when they were working on a cooking badge. She went home without it, and when her mother asked where it was, Nellie said she thought she saw Mrs. Norton put it in her coat pocket."

"Why would she do that?" Dawn asked.

"That's not the end of the story," Piper said.

"Oops, sorry," Dawn said.

"Thelma told Nellie that if Mrs. Norton wanted the recipe box, then she probably needed it more than they did. 'There are plenty of recipes in the world,' Thelma said, 'and one of the best is for kindness. Kindness calls for friendliness, helpfulness, patience, and putting yourself in someone else's shoes.' And Nellie said, 'Or their coat pocket?' And Thelma said, 'Exactly.' Nellie put the quilt squares in the trunk, and the recipe box wrapped in her mother Joyce's apron, so that both her mothers would be together."

"You can recite that word for word?" Debbie asked with a smile.

Piper nodded. "Because it's such a good story."

"Both her mothers," Dawn said softly. "Did Nellie put the clothes in the trunk?"

"Her father did," Piper said. "He left Nellie and Barbara a note about it in the trunk. Nellie didn't find the trunk until after Barbara died."

"I don't remember seeing that note in the trunk," Janet said.

"Nellie told me about it but she didn't show it to me," Piper said.

"Too personal," Dawn said.

"Yeah." Piper sighed. "She said her father told her he'd listened to advice from well-meaning people, who said that unless he erased Joyce from the house the memories would be too painful. They told him it would be better for Nellie and the new baby."

Dawn made an incredulous noise. "What a cruel idea."

"Right?" Piper said. "His note said he couldn't bear to part with everything, so he packed some of Joyce's favorite clothes and her diary in the trunk with the note. Nellie said even though she loved Thelma like a mother, and knew Thelma loved her, when she found the trunk she felt like she'd found a connection to her first mother again."

"Maybe," Janet said, "the wedding dress was the most special item of all to him and he's the one who put it in the hidden compartment of the trunk. And maybe that's why Nellie left it there, out of respect for her father. I guess we'll never know."

"Makes you think, doesn't it?" Dawn said.

"What are you thinking?" Debbie asked.

"About how my husband and I never could understand why Nellie liked this town so much. Maybe that's because we never spent enough time here. Or enough time with her."

"Sometimes that can't be helped," Courtney said. "Lives are busy. Are you putting the house on the market?"

"That was the original plan," Dawn said.

"Do I sense a 'but'?" Janet asked.

Dawn looked around the table. "I'm kind of in the groove of clearing houses out at this point. I might have to think about making a clean sweep of the house in Yellow Springs and start over in Dennison. If I did, I'd be halfway closer to my grandchildren in Cincinnati. Then I'd be in a good place, figuratively and literally."

"I think that calls for dessert all around," Debbie said. "Does anyone object to chocolate? No? My kind of people. Give me a hand, Janet?"

"Sure thing." Janet heard the buzz of a text arriving for one of the guests as she followed Debbie to the kitchen. Glancing over her shoulder, she saw a frown come and go from Kim's face as she looked at her phone.

"None for me, Debbie," Kim said, coming into the kitchen. "This was great, delicious, revelatory, and all the rest, but you know. Big program tomorrow. Big nerves and getting bigger tonight. I'm going to slip out the back door. Say good night to the others for me."

"I heard the text," Janet said. "Everything okay?"

"From Renee," Kim said, her face looking tight. "She said, 'My incontrovertible proof beats yours. See you tomorrow.'"

"But it can't," Janet said.

"It can't," Kim agreed. "But what happens if she refuses to be convinced? Correction. *When* she refuses to be convinced. I have a bad feeling about this."

CHAPTER THIRTY

Rather than roll over and go back to sleep Saturday morning, when Janet's alarm rang, she jumped out of bed and went downstairs to make a pot of coffee. Ian soon joined her.

"Your fashion show is today. May it be a huge success," he said, "the audience enrapt, and every last crumb of food eaten with gusto."

"Gusto—that'll be great. Are you sure you don't want to come see a bevy of pretty women in adorable clothes?"

"I'm married to the only pretty woman I care about. When the show's a wrap, will you feel like the mysteries surrounding the trunk are solved? Are you satisfied?"

Janet had kept him up-to-date as they solved the puzzles piece by piece. "Except for the mystery of why Renee Peterson is so sure the wedding dress belonged to her grandmother. We've wondered about ulterior motives. We know, for a fact, the dress belonged to Nellie's mother, Joyce. Kim told Renee that. Until the email arrived from her, last night, Kim hoped she'd quietly dropped the idea."

"I don't see our fearless museum director fighting a duel over the dress, but if things go south, use your speed dial. I'm at your call."

"I'm sure it'll be fine. As for being satisfied, yes, I think I am. I started out wishing I'd taken the time to know Nellie better. Then I wished I'd known about her hobby of finishing unfinished objects.

Then I realized that I, and all her students, walked out of her class at the end of the year more finished than we'd been when we first walked in."

"An interesting take on teachers," Ian said. "But, yeah, the best ones fill our brains and our lives."

"Exactly. And finding the clues and filling in the blanks to solve the mysteries has been like finishing one of Nellie's UFOs. *Very* satisfying."

"Where is Kim Smith?" a ringing voice demanded.

Janet and Debbie, who were talking to Piper and Courtney outside the workroom designated as the fashion show's dressing room, turned to see Renee Peterson, fists on her hips.

"Uh-oh," Debbie breathed. "An hour to showtime, and it looks like a different show just started."

"Maybe we can head her off." Janet didn't really believe her own words.

"Um, Janet, I'm holding the wedding dress," Debbie said.

Catching sight of them, Renee stalked over. "Get Kim. That dress belonged to my grandmother. I have incontrovertible photographic proof. That makes it mine."

Piper looked at Renee curiously. "Nellie didn't have children, so you must be Dawn's daughter."

"I'm not."

Piper took a step back.

"I'll text Kim," Janet said.

Courtney nodded down the corridor. "She's already on her way."

"It's nice to see you, Renee," Kim said pleasantly when she arrived.

Renee pulled a photograph from her purse and waved it in Kim's face. "Incontrovertible photographic proof."

Kim held out her hand. "May I hold it so I can see it?" she asked. "No."

"Then will you hold it still?" Kim asked. "Thanks."

Janet, Debbie, Piper, and Courtney crowded around Kim. The photo, a grainy black and white with scalloped edges, showed a young woman holding a dress that looked amazingly like the dress Debbie held.

"Wow." Kim looked from the photo to the dress in front of her. "It's uncanny. As I said in my email, though, our dress belonged to Joyce Terrell. Her grandmother made it. We can prove it, and you have no legal claim on this dress."

"I will take you to court."

"Renee, the dress is the grand finale of the fashion show," Kim said. "Let's continue this conversation afterward."

Renee looked Kim up and down. "I don't want someone stuffed into the dress and splitting its seams."

"Debbie is wearing it," Kim said. "It fits her like it was made for her."

"I don't care. I don't want to take the chance that my grand-mother's precious dress will be ruined. You're serving food, right? So what if someone reaches out as Debbie walks past and touches it with greasy fingers? I want to take it with me now."

Janet hoped her own face didn't show her thoughts—greasy fingers? To be fair, there might be *messy* fingers.

"You're right to be concerned," Courtney said. "I'm the emcee for the show, and I've already planned to ask the audience not to reach out and touch the clothes. I'll remind them of that when Debbie wears the dress."

"That's a great idea, Courtney," Kim said. "Renee, we understand your concerns. But at the moment, the dress is the possession of the museum, we're in the process of getting ready for a much-anticipated program, and the dress is a major part."

"Kim?" Janet said. "Maybe Renee could join the audience, free of charge, to keep an eye on things?"

"You mean watch someone else wear my grandmother's dress? *That's* a hard no."

"Okay," Kim said. "No problem."

Janet liked Kim's calm manner. She *didn't* like the smoldering look on Renee's face and wondered how volatile she was. It might be a good idea…. Janet pulled out her phone, turned her back to Renee, and made a quick, quiet call to Ian.

"After the program," Kim was saying when Janet turned back, "I'll be perfectly happy to show you the information we have about the dress. For now, and meaning no disrespect, we're in the middle of things and on a tight schedule."

"I know disrespect when I hear it," Renee said. "I'm calling the police."

"Renee?" Janet held up her phone. "I just did."

Renee looked momentarily confused but recovered quickly. "Perfect," she said. "I'm glad *someone* here has sense."

Piper whispered something to Courtney. Courtney listened, her mouth briefly falling open. She squeezed Piper's shoulder then used a used a voice very much like Nellie Lightwood's when she wanted the undivided attention of every student within earshot. "May I look at the photograph more closely?"

Renee grudgingly handed the photo to her. Courtney studied the photo, eyes going back and forth between it and the dress Debbie still held.

"It really is uncanny," Courtney said to Kim. She looked at Renee. "The buttons in the photo are slightly larger, though, and the darts are nearer the buttons on the dress Debbie is holding."

"Baloney." Renee no longer smoldered. She looked molten.

"But Renee?" Courtney said. "Piper and I think we recognize your grandmother's dress. It's in our costume collection at the high school." She checked the time. "If Piper and I go now, we can bring the dress back before the fashion show starts."

"Hey, look who's here," Janet said, waving to Ian as he came down the hall toward them.

Renee turned to see then pivoted back to Janet with a sour expression. "Not Courtney and Piper."

"My husband," Janet said. "But the others will be back before you know it." She was glad to see Ian's smiling face. She'd called and let him know the situation was calm while they waited for a second wedding dress to arrive. He'd assured her he would be over before long anyway. She was grateful for that, because Renee had complained constantly while refusing to make the wait more comfortable by sitting down in Kim's office.

"Afternoon, all," Ian said. "Kim, Debbie, nice to see you. I'm looking forward to the fashion show."

"You are?" Janet said. "But you decided against it. You don't have a ticket."

"I couldn't resist and decided to surprise you."

"He was lucky," Kim said. "He got the last ticket a few days ago. You're a bit early, Ian."

"Answering a duty call." Ian held his hand out to Renee. "I don't believe we've met. I'm Janet's husband, Ian. Also known as Police Chief Shaw."

Renee gave Kim a triumphant look. "I'm glad you're here. I'm Renee Peterson. If you don't mind waiting here with me, I might need to report a theft to you."

"I'll stand by, but first, do you feel you're in danger, Ms. Peterson?"

"What? No. Why?"

"There's no need for alarm," Ian said. "I'm just making sure I know what I'm dealing with."

"Good. Thank you for taking me seriously." Renee shot another look at Kim.

"Here come Courtney and Piper," Debbie said, sounding relieved.

Courtney walked quickly up to them carrying a garment bag. Piper, grinning, trotted beside her. Janet watched Renee's face and saw hope beginning to replace her anger.

"Debbie?" Courtney said. "Will you bring the museum's dress here?" She unzipped the garment bag, removed the theater department's dress, and handed it, on its hanger, to Piper. Debbie and Piper held the two dresses side by side.

"Amazing," Courtney studied the dresses. "They're so much alike. They're both homemade, so the seamstresses might have bought the same or similar patterns. Still, the darts and buttons are different."

Renee looked from one dress to the other then from her photograph to both dresses again. Finally, she pointed at the theater department's dress. "It's…it's—" That was as far as she got before bursting into tears.

Kim handed Renee tissues and gave her a hug.

"I owe you such a big apology," Renee said.

"How about answers to a few questions too?" Janet asked. "The first day you came into the café, why did you lie and say you had an appointment with Kim?"

Renee blushed. "For a stupid reason. Nothing about me is special. My grandmother was special. Her dress was. I'd been looking for her dress off and on since she passed. When I thought I'd found it, and I came to get it, I wanted to make the whole day special and important, and what sounds more important than saying you have an appointment with the director of a museum? I wasn't even on a real phone call. I faked it. But I didn't fake how important my grandmother was to me."

"Why didn't you make a real appointment?" Kim asked.

"I was afraid you'd say no. Instead you've all been nothing but kind."

"One more question," Janet said, "then we need to scoot. Where did you go for the couple of hours between leaving the café and stopping at the museum that day?"

"Visiting my grandmother's grave. Courtney, may I buy the dress from you?"

"Oh, Renee, there's no need for that." Courtney turned to Piper. "What do you think, Piper?"

"That Nellie would have done this." Piper put the dress in Renee's arms.

A large group came from Good Shepherd for the show. Janet helped Clary and Rita fix plates at the laden buffet table and carry them to their seats. She didn't see Eileen, which worried her. However, Kim was here, there, and everywhere, ensuring that models were dressed and everything else was running smoothly. Rather than try to catch Kim and ask about Eileen, Janet said a quick prayer for her continued good health. Harry and Patricia caught her eye and waved. Paulette, true to her word, had brought Dorothy Simms. Greg had come too, and Ian slipped into the seat next to him. Dawn waved at Janet and sat next to Dorothy, chatting happily. Janet, standing near the buffet table, was pleased to see they had a full house.

Courtney stepped out in front of the audience. "Welcome to the Dennison Railroad Depot Museum's first-ever fashion show, which would not be possible without Dawn Anderson's generous donation of a trunk full of clothes. It was also a trunk full of mysteries, it turns out. You'll learn a little bit about that during our show today. Shall we begin?"

The first model appeared and walked down the improvised runway.

"Our first model is wearing a pleated skirt and top combo that's a cute variation on a sailor theme. Note the top's square yoke and hip pockets," Courtney said. "The impact of the war can be seen in the style and silhouette of the clothing our models are wearing, and in a new simplicity. Utility clothing became the fashion. Simpler silhouettes to conserve fabric. Limited clasps, buttons, and zippers to conserve metal. And man-made fibers to save silk and wool for the military." She gave a nod, and the first model stepped to the side. Piper was next up.

"Piper is wearing a darling, bright yellow playsuit. Note the dropped shoulder yokes with gathers—a common feature in the early '40s that was also seen in the classic shirtwaist dress, a style that had its heyday in the 1940s but hasn't gone out of style since." She nodded again to the queue of woman waiting their turn.

"Speaking of shirtwaist dresses, here comes our next model in a robin's-egg blue shirtwaist covered in big white polka dots. Notice her hat and gloves. Doesn't she look a picture?"

Model after model walked the runway, showing off Joyce Lightwood's favorite clothes—dresses, skirts, blouses, trousers, a hand-knitted sweater—many of them made by her or her grandmother. Courtney sprinkled snippets of Joyce's story throughout her narration.

Toward the end of the program, Kim joined Janet by the buffet table. Kim looked like the cat that swallowed the canary.

"You're up to something," Janet whispered.

"Shh."

Janet turned back to the runway, and her hand flew to her mouth. Eileen walked down the runway escorted by Ray in his World War II uniform. Eileen wore her own trousers and a soft cotton top, but over them she wore a reproduction of the apron they'd found in the trunk.

"Kim!" Janet said.

"Shh."

Eileen looked like she was in seventh heaven. Ray beamed. The applause was deafening.

"I made two more aprons," Kim said. "One for you, one for Debbie. Now hush. Here she comes."

"Our last model, Debbie, is wearing the wedding dress that Joyce Lightwood's grandmother made for her." Courtney told the story of the blizzard and the wedding.

Janet, only half listening, watched the faces of the audience as they followed Debbie's walk along the runway. Janet didn't see a single person in the room who wasn't enjoying the event. And to think all this started when they opened the trunk. Or had it started when Dawn found the trunk in the attic crawl space? No, she realized, it started with Nellie Lightwood. Nellie, a wise and kind woman, who learned from her parents to leave a margin for the unexpected. Nellie, who left gifts for her friends, neighbors, and complete strangers so they would find joy in unexpected places.

In trying to solve the mysteries and reconnect with Nellie, Janet knew that Nellie had taught her one last lesson—that spreading kindness and joy is like spreading sunshine. She vowed to continue living that lesson in her own life.

Debbie neared the end of the runway, approaching Greg, whose seat was front and center. She looked completely comfortable. Confident and radiant, her skirts rustled gently as she walked. And Greg—Greg had eyes only for Debbie in the beautiful wedding dress.

Janet nudged Kim. "How soon do you think we'll hear wedding bells ringing in Dennison?"

Dear Reader,

I had so much fun filling the trunk that Dawn donated to the Dennison Railroad Depot Museum! I've always wanted to find a trunk like it—can picture the attic so clearly, smell the dust and the rafters, would really like to find that little door and crawl inside with a flashlight.

The recipe for dream bars that Janet found in the recipe box could easily have come from the old blue stationery box I keep safely in a drawer. The box is full of recipes my grandmother wrote out or clipped from newspapers starting in the early 1900s. My granny's recipes tend toward savory dishes, though, so I gave the dream bars recipe to Janet's grandmother (and also gave her my grandmother's last name). The recipe was first published on Friday, May 4, 1934, in the *Lincoln Star*, by Mrs. Edna Whitmus of Sargent, Nebraska.

I also have Joyce's flour sacking apron. Like the apron in the trunk, mine is fragile. It belonged to my great-aunt Bess. There are a few holes and stains, and the fabric has obviously been washed often, but the colors are still so right for the Whistle Stop Café!

Years ago I was the curator, and then director, of the history museum in Tennessee's oldest town: Jonesborough. We had beautiful examples of signature quilts in the collection. Reading the embroidered names of the quilters sent little shivers down my spine—each quilt had a story, and each name did too.

The most fun of all came in choosing clothes for the trunk. I read articles about fashion during the war years and learned how styles changed as part of the war effort. I looked at ads in magazines and newspapers from the early '40s, at Butterick sewing patterns, and the trove of photographs available on the internet. The best photographs, though, are the ones I have of my mother and father. They married in June 1941, so, unlike Joyce and Theo, they had the luxury of time together before Dad shipped out for the China, India, Burma Theater in late 1942. I have three or four pictures of them looking so young and happy. One of the pictures is of their small wedding. Is Mom wearing the dress that Joyce's Gran made for her? I think she is.

Thank you for joining Janet, Debbie, and me in another Whistle Stop Café Mystery. I love the feeling of community that develops in a long-running series—the community of characters *in* the stories and the wider community of the readers who enjoy the stories. Thank you for being among them.

Warm wishes and happy reading,
Margaret Welch

ABOUT the AUTHOR

Margaret Welch loves cats, cooking, and crossword puzzles, but she especially loves everything about books. She enjoys writing mystery fiction and loves traveling by train. Margaret has lived in Illinois, Wisconsin, Texas, Tennessee, and Scotland.

A GLIMPSE *of the* PAST

Flour Sack Fashions for Victory

Don't you love the stories of folks on the home front pulling together during World War II? Until working on the Whistle Stop Café Mysteries, I hadn't known what role flour and feed sacks played in those stories. During the Depression, clothes sewn from sacking material carried the stigma of rural poverty. But as rationing came into effect during the war, urban and suburban women were encouraged to join their thrifty rural sisters in the patriotic reuse of feed and flour sacks. The Textile Bag Manufacturers Association boosted this move with a new slogan: "A yard of material saved is a yard gained for victory."

In 1943, when the War Production Board restricted the use of cotton print cloth to military and industrial uses, yard goods and ready-to-wear house dresses became scarce in shops. Commodity sacks, however, were classified as "industrial." Commodity sack manufacturers had already been producing cotton percale bags for chicken feed, flour, sugar, salt, and meal in bright colors and printed designs, so women had plenty of new places to shop for dressmaking materials—feed stores, bakeries, groceries, and farmer's markets.

To aid the war effort, bag sizes were standardized to 100, 50, 25, 10, 5, and 2 pounds, making it easier for millers and housewives to estimate material needed. For instance, to make a dress requiring three yards of fabric, a woman needed two or three hundred-pound flour sacks, depending on the dress pattern and the pattern of the fabric. Clothing items requiring less fabric became trendy, creating slimmer, shorter skirts and dresses.

Manufacturers made the bags easy to reuse too. They chain-stitched the bags along one side and across the bottom so the entire line of stitching could be pulled out quickly (and a truly thrifty woman saved that string!). Some manufacturers printed patterns for dolls and doll clothes on the backs of the bags. Other bags came pre-hemmed so they could be turned into an apron or tablecloth quite easily after the chain stitching was removed. If women had bags they didn't want or need, they might sell them for much-needed cash. Women also hosted bag parties, where they exchanged bags with friends, and they traded bags at home demonstration clubs.

Sacking was a versatile, well-made cotton fabric. During the war, the resourceful community of stitchers made dresses, aprons, petticoats, hair bows, pants, children's overalls, shorts, shirts, under-wear, diapers, curtains, bedspreads, quilts, and dish towels (lots of dish towels—there were no automatic dishwashers, so everyone dried dishes). The home front women of World War II could have seen their reliance on flour sack fashions as another deprivation of the terrible war, or they could have stood proudly and seen their reused cotton couture as a symbol of President Franklin D. Roosevelt's "We can...we will...we must!" patriotism. Which vision do you think they chose?

FROM the HOME-FRONT KITCHEN

Grandma Faye's Dream Bars

Ingredients:

Crust

½ cup butter, softened

½ cup brown sugar, packed

1 cup all-purpose flour

Topping

2 large eggs

1 cup brown sugar, packed

2 tablespoons all-purpose flour

½ teaspoon baking powder

½ teaspoon salt

1 cup sweetened flaked coconut

1 cup chopped nutmeats
   (pecans or walnuts work well)

1 teaspoon vanilla extract

Directions:

To make crust:

Preheat oven to 350°F. Janet's grandmother didn't have parchment paper, but if you do, line your pan with enough parchment so the ends come up and over the sides (this way you'll be able to lift your dream bars out of the pan easily). Grease the parchment.

Cream together butter and brown sugar. Add flour and mix until just combined.

Press into prepared pan and bake 10 to 15 minutes, until starting to turn golden. Remove from oven and let cool while you prepare topping.

To make topping:

Mix together flour, salt, and baking powder. Stir in coconut and nutmeats.

Beat together eggs, sugar, salt, and baking powder. Stir in dry ingredients. Stir in vanilla.

Spread mixture over crust and bake 20 to 25 minutes, until dream bars are starting to turn golden.

Cool in pan for 10 minutes. Lift uncut bars from pan and let cool completely before cutting.

*Read on for a sneak peek of another exciting book
in the* Whistle Stop Café Mysteries *series!*

NOW YOU'RE IN
MY ARMS

by Leslie Gould

appy February!" Debbie Albright called out as she opened the back door of the Whistle Stop Café. She stomped her boots and then stepped over the threshold. "Can you believe this snow? It's close to a half foot already." She pulled the door closed against the storm.

Janet Shaw, Debbie's best friend, stepped out of the kitchen, wearing a white apron adorned with red and pink hearts. She held up an identical apron for Debbie and grinned. "Happy February to you too!"

Debbie clapped her gloved hands together and gave Janet a hearty "Thank you!"

Debbie had always loved February. January was over. Valentine's Day was only two weeks away, which meant decorating sugar cookies and making homemade valentines. This year, for the second year in a row, plans for the Valentine's Day Dance were in full swing.

And for the first Valentine's Day in twenty-two years, she had a sweetheart. Yes, her romance with Greg Connor just kept getting better and better.

February was going to be an amazing month.

A half hour later, Debbie flipped the Open sign. An hour after that, she and Janet sat at the counter. "I didn't expect it to be this slow," Janet said.

"Business might still pick up." Debbie wrapped her hands around her hot mug of coffee. "If not, we knew there would be days like this. And it's certainly not the first time. Remember last month's storm?" Buying the café together had been a risk for the two lifelong friends— one that usually paid off.

Janet glanced out the window at the large, falling snowflakes and then back at Debbie. "Let's talk about the dance. How about if we host an event next Saturday to make decorations for the lobby? I have a box of doilies and old cards we can use. We'll decorate the depot lobby for the entire month with what people make."

"Sounds lovely." Debbie took a sip of coffee.

"I was going through photographs of last year's dance that Kim gave me from the museum collection and thought it would be fun to make a display," Janet said. "I'll print the photos in black and white and use black paper and photo corners to make it look like a 1940s scrapbook. Then I can mount them on a tri-fold board."

"Perfect!" Debbie loved how creative Janet was, and not just with her baking.

The front door to the café dinged. A couple Debbie didn't recognize stepped inside.

Debbie slid off her stool and reached for two menus. "Welcome!" she said as she started toward them.

The next customer through the door was Harry Franklin with his dog, Crosby, trailing behind him. "Harry, what are you doing out in this snow?" Debbie gently chided, then grabbed a mug and the coffeepot. He was a young ninety-seven years, but he still shouldn't be risking a fall.

"You can't keep me away from a hearty breakfast and a good cup of coffee." He grinned.

"Is Patricia joining you?" Patricia Franklin was his doting granddaughter.

"Not this morning." He sat at his usual table. "Her car's in the shop."

"How was the walk over?" Debbie asked.

"Just fine. People are shoveling their sidewalks. The snow is fluffy—not icy. I didn't have a problem." He reached down to pet the dog. "Neither did Crosby."

Paulette, Greg's widowed mother who was also a server at the café, came in at nine and joined Debbie and Janet in the kitchen. Greg's father, EJ, had died years ago.

"Goodness," Paulette said. "What a morning." She took off her coat. "I stopped by my storage unit to retrieve the rest of the boxes full of stuff Jaxon helped me go through. There are a couple of boxes that belonged to my mother-in-law I want to give to Greg. EJ ended up with a lot of Vivian's things. I was going to give everything to his sister Sally, but when her husband died she downsized to an apartment at Good Shepherd." Paulette took a deep breath. It wasn't like her to talk so quickly. "Anyway, when I arrived at Greg's, I realized

I'd forgotten my key. He's at the basketball tournament with Jaxon, and Julian spent the night at a friend's house. I had to trudge around to the back porch and leave the boxes there, in the enclosed part." Her eyes twinkled. "I don't know what I was thinking, clearing out the rest of my storage unit on a day like today."

Debbie gave her a sympathetic look. She would have been happy to help.

As Paulette hung up her coat, Janet said, "There's a new apron for you on your hook."

Debbie put her arm around Janet. "It matches ours."

"How fun." Paulette grabbed her new apron, pulled it over her dark hair, and struck a pose, followed by a grin.

Business gradually picked up and held steady until just before two—an hour before closing—when the last customer left. Janet left soon after, and then Debbie shooed Paulette, who needed to get her giveaway boxes to the thrift store, out the door. Then she texted Greg.

How's the tournament going?

He texted back, Great! The last game just ended. We won. See you at swing dance class. They'd signed up for a refresher course to be ready for the Valentine's Day event.

Debbie "loved" his text and slipped her phone into her pocket. There was no one in the world she'd rather dance with than Greg.

As Debbie flipped the sign to Closed, Kim Smith, curator of the Dennison Depot Museum, stepped through the front door and asked, "Do you have a minute?"

"Sure." Debbie straightened the sign. "What's up?"

"I'm working on an exhibit about women on the home front and wanted to feature a war widow from the area. I thought of Greg's grandmother. Paulette said one time that her mother-in-law belonged to the church knitting circle and made socks, gloves, and scarves—that sort of thing—for the soldiers. I'd love to feature her. Do you think Greg or Paulette have photographs and a couple of artifacts we could use?"

"Paulette just dropped off a couple of boxes of Vivian's things at Greg's today, so maybe."

"Would you mind asking him?" Kim's voice wavered. "And perhaps help me with that part of the exhibit?"

Debbie tilted her head. "Is everything okay?"

"I think so. Barry hasn't been feeling well and had a round of tests yesterday. Just now, I realized I'm more stressed than I thought."

Debbie reached for her friend's hand. "Of course I'll help."

"Thank you."

"I know how much you're looking forward to the dance on Valentine's Day," Debbie said. "I hope the doctor can sort out Barry's medical concerns by then."

"So do I." Kim's eyes grew teary. "He's been having an irregular heartbeat." She blinked the tears away. "Dancing might be out, and I don't want to dance without him."

Debbie gave Kim a hug and then said, "Greg and I signed up for the refresher class at the community center. It starts this afternoon. I'll ask him about you featuring his grandmother in the exhibit and let you know."

After Kim headed back to the museum, Debbie got to work cleaning the café and prepping for Monday morning. Then she headed home. The snow had stopped falling and the sun had come out, creating a sparkly white landscape. As she made her way down the shoveled sidewalks, she breathed in the crisp air. By the time she reached her bungalow, she was a little chilled. After turning up the heat, she made herself a cup of tea and called her mother. Her parents lived just outside of town.

After saying hello, Debbie asked, "How are you and Dad doing with the snow?"

"Just fine, although I have a little bit of a cold. We're going to miss church tomorrow."

Debbie gave her mom a synopsis of her day. After the two caught up, Debbie said, "Let me know if you need anything." They said their goodbyes, and Debbie ended the call.

She thought about Kim's request. There didn't seem to be a reason to wait to ask in person, so why not text Greg now about Kim wanting to include his grandmother in her upcoming home-front exhibit and asking Debbie to help with it?

Debbie sent the text, opened the novel she'd started yesterday, and sipped her tea. Fifteen minutes later, Greg responded.

I'D BE HONORED IF KIM INCLUDED GRANDMA. IN FACT, I JUST DROPPED JAXON OFF AT THE HOUSE AND HE FOUND TWO BOXES MOM LEFT ON THE BACK PORCH. I'M OFF TO CHECK A WORK SITE. LET'S MEET AT THE COMMUNITY HALL. DON'T FORGET YOUR DANCING SHOES!

Debbie replied, I CAN'T WAIT TO FIND OUT MORE ABOUT YOUR GRANDMOTHER. AND TO PUT ON MY DANCING SHOES. She sent Kim a confirmation message, and then went upstairs to change.

When she arrived at the community hall, Greg's pickup wasn't in the parking lot. She went on inside, sat in a chair along the perimeter of the hall, and changed out of her boots into her shoes. Then she took off her long coat. She wore an A-line, knee-length sapphire blue dress with a full skirt. It was one of a few dresses she owned that worked for swing dancing. Spinning around as the skirt flared always made her feel like a girl again.

More dancers congregated, and one of the instructors started the music. The leader appeared to be in her late fifties. "Welcome!" The woman gestured. "Please gather around."

Debbie glanced toward the door. Where was Greg? She joined the other students in a half circle around the instructors.

The woman said, "I'm Meg Sinclair." She looked familiar. Debbie had definitely seen her around town. Meg wore a bright red dress, matching lipstick, and black pumps. She'd piled her blondish-gray hair on top of her head.

She motioned to the man next to her. "And this is my husband, Jeff."

He gave a wave as he smiled. Jeff appeared to be a few years older than Meg, and he looked familiar too.

"We took up swing dancing thirty years ago," Meg said. "We taught classes here for years and recently decided to do it again."

The door opened and Greg stepped into the hall, giving Debbie a smile. Relieved, she waved. Then he sat down to change into his dancing shoes.

Meg explained more about the class and just as she asked the men to form a line on the far end of the hall and the women on the near end, Greg was at Debbie's side. He gave her a half hug and followed the other men.

Jeff and Meg demonstrated the rock step, a basic move where the dancer steps forward with one foot then steps back with the other. Jeff then stood with his back to the men and Meg stood facing him, leading the students in practice. Next they worked on triple steps to the left and triple steps to the right.

Debbie kept her eyes on Greg, who looked as handsome as ever in his black slacks and blue button-down shirt.

Meg switched the music to Glenn Miller's "In the Mood" and told everyone to find a partner. Greg took five quick steps to Debbie's side. She turned to him. He placed a hand on her lower back, and she placed a hand on his shoulder. He clasped her free hand with his. Greg met Debbie's eyes and grinned.

As Meg and Jeff stepped into position, Meg called out, "Rock step. Release your partner. Rock backward and outward for the two triple steps, extending your arm…"

"Aha." Debbie drew her arm in. "I remember where I saw Meg and Jeff before—at the Valentine's Dance a year ago."

Greg had a puzzled expression on his face.

"Do you remember them?"

He shook his head.

Debbie did. They definitely knew what they were doing then—and now.

Meg called out, "Triple step."

Greg stepped, and Debbie followed. Or tried to. She stepped on Greg's foot. He laughed and added an extra quick step.

Debbie cringed. "Sorry."

"That's okay," Greg said. "You can step on my foot anytime."

Meg called out, "Rock step."

Greg and Debbie glided through the next several moves but then she stepped on Greg's foot again.

"Sorry," she said again.

"Don't worry about it." Greg replaced his hand on Debbie's back. "I was off a beat."

After the class, Greg kept hold of Debbie's hand. "You did great. I'm a little rusty though."

"No," Debbie answered. "I'm the one who stepped on your feet."

Greg led her to the chairs. "Want to come by for a while? You could help me go through Grandma's boxes and see if there's anything Kim can use in the exhibit. Julian made chili this afternoon, and Jaxon said he'd make corn bread. The boys are making dinner."

"Sure," Debbie said. "I'd like that."

When they reached Greg's house, he took Debbie's arm and held tight as they walked up the icy steps. Greg opened the front door and Debbie stepped in first, inhaling the spicy aroma.

"I'm home," Greg called out. "Debbie's here too!"

Julian, who was in the eighth grade, dashed out of the kitchen. "Hi, Dad! Hi, Debbie. The chili's ready." He tore past them and up the open staircase.

"Did Jaxon start the corn bread?" Greg called out after him.

"Noooo!" Julian's voice faded as he reached the landing.

After they hung up their coats, Greg called up the stairs, "Jaxon, would you start the corn bread, please?"

A moment later, Jaxon came thundering down the stairs. "Sorry. After I shoveled the snow, I got distracted by the Ohio State game. They're playing Indiana." He slid into the kitchen in his stocking feet.

"Thanks for doing it now," Greg called after him. He motioned to the two cardboard boxes on the glass-top coffee table in the living room and said to Debbie, "We might as well go through these before dinner."

Debbie nodded and sat down on the sofa. Greg sat next to her and pulled a box closer. He took his keychain from his pocket, opened up his small Swiss Army knife, and cut the packing tape. Then he reached inside and pulled out a piece of paper. After a moment he smiled. "Mom made an inventory list. This box is all diaries from 1939 to 1985."

"No family treasures?" Debbie teased. "Although these are treasures in their own way."

Greg chuckled. "The fanciest thing Grandma owned was her wedding ring."

"From your Grandpa Earl or Grandpa Ted?" Earl had gone off to war, leaving Greg's grandmother with four children when he was killed in combat. Later, she had married Ted Johnston, who had served with Earl overseas and was the only father Greg's dad, EJ—Earl Junior—had ever known.

Greg furrowed his brow. "I'm guessing from Grandpa Ted." He lifted out a diary and opened it. "This is the first one." He turned the book toward Debbie. "She started it the day my aunt Sally, her first child, was born in 1938." He leafed through the pages. "The first entry is full of emotion, then the next few are mostly about the weather and farm work. Lots of facts."

"But few feelings?"

"Looks that way," he said.

"Not everyone can express their emotions, even in the pages of a private diary. Perhaps she was just more comfortable recording daily events."

"That makes sense. Especially when you consider she had four children and worked on a farm. I'm surprised she had time to do even this much." He returned the diary to the box.

"These will take a while to go through," Debbie said. "But I can narrow it down by focusing only on the dates during the war."

Greg reached for the second box and one flap popped up as he gripped it. He opened the box and retrieved the inventory list. "Photographs and letters." He lifted out a stack of envelopes. "These are from Grandpa Earl." He pulled out another packet. "And these are Grandma's letters to him." Then he fished out a single envelope. "This is from Grandpa Ted, postmarked November 1946."

He searched in the box a moment more and came up with a third packet. "These are all from someone named Daisy Chapman." He slid the top envelope from the stack and opened it. "It's signed 'your sister, Daisy.'" He frowned. "I didn't know Grandma had a sister named Daisy—or any sister at all."

"How odd," Debbie said. "Maybe Daisy was just a friend, but they were close as sisters."

Greg looked thoughtful. "Maybe. It will take quite a bit of time to go through the letters." He set the last packet next to the other ones on the coffee table. "But let's look at the photographs now. We can put anything from the World War II era aside for you to show to Kim, same as the diaries, and get you two started on your project."

Debbie reached into the box and pulled out a stack of photos. For the next fifteen minutes they sorted through pictures that ranged from the mid-1930s to the late 1980s and weren't in any sort of chronological order. Fortunately, most had a date stamped on the bottom.

When the timer rang for the corn bread, Greg put down his stack of photographs and headed into the kitchen while Debbie reached into the box to see if there was anything else. Her hand bumped against something soft and round.

She stood and looked into the box. At the bottom was a ball of yarn still attached to a scarf that hadn't been finished. One needle was attached to the last row. She smiled. Just last month, she and Janet had solved a mystery involving a person who was completing people's unfinished projects and blessing random Dennison residents with her handiwork.

Perhaps this scarf was one Vivian had been making for a soldier for the war effort, if not for Earl himself. But wouldn't she have finished it?

Debbie checked Paulette's inventory. There was no mention of the scarf.

The yarn was thick and uneven and a grayish white. As she examined it more closely, she noticed odd sequences of stitches in the scarf, a mix of purl and knit stitches in multiple rows. She knew little about knitting, but it didn't look right. The needle fell out of the ball of yarn, and Debbie thrust it back in—hitting something in the middle that wouldn't allow the needle to go through. She dug her finger around, but the ball was tightly wound and she didn't make much progress.

Greg stepped into the living room. "What's that?"

Debbie held up the ball. "There's something in the middle." She started unwinding the ball. After a few minutes and a big pile of loose yarn, a ring with an enormous stone fell into her lap.

She picked it up. "Does this look familiar?"

"No," Greg said. "I've never seen it before. But I don't imagine it's worth anything. My grandmother was a farmer's wife. She didn't have expensive jewelry."

The stone did seem dull. The metal was in good shape and not tarnished at all. Small stones stretched halfway around the band on each side. As the ring caught the light, the big stone shimmered a little. She glanced up at Greg. "You should get this appraised just in case it's not costume jewelry. But even costume jewelry can be valuable, if it's by certain designers."

He nodded. "I wonder where it came from. And why was it in the middle of a ball of yarn?"

A NOTE FROM the EDITORS

We hope you enjoyed another exciting volume in the Whistle Stop Café Mysteries series, published by Guideposts. For over seventy-five years, Guideposts, a nonprofit organization, has been driven by a vision of a world filled with hope. We aspire to be the voice of a trusted friend, a friend who makes you feel more hopeful and connected.

By making a purchase from Guideposts, you join our community in touching millions of lives, inspiring them to believe that all things are possible through faith, hope, and prayer. Your continued support allows us to provide uplifting resources to those in need. Whether through our communities, websites, apps, or publications, we inspire our audiences, bring them together, and comfort, uplift, entertain, and guide them. Visit us at guideposts.org to learn more.

We would love to hear from you. Write us at Guideposts, P.O. Box 5815, Harlan, Iowa 51593 or call us at (800) 932-2145. Did you love *Wait Till the Sun Shines*? Leave a review for this product on guideposts.org/shop. Your feedback helps others in our community find relevant products.